CRYSTALS FOR POSITIVE MANIFESTATION

CRYSTALS FOR POSITIVE MANIFESTATION

A Practical Sourcebook of 100 Crystals

Sarah Bartlett

FAIR WINDS

Quarto is the authority on a wide range of topics.

Quarto educates, entertains and enriches the lives of our readers—enthusiasts and lovers of hands-on living.

www.QuartoKnows.com

First published in the United States of America in 2017 by
Fair Winds Press, an imprint of
The Quarto Group
100 Cummings Center
Suite 265-D
Beverly, Massachusetts 01915-6101
Telephone: (978) 282-9590
Fax: (978) 283-2742
QuartoKnows.com
Visit our blogs at QuartoKnows.com

10 9 8 7 6 5 4 3 2 1

ISBN: 978-1-59233-768-8

Conceived, designed, and produced by
Quid Publishing
Level One Ouvest House
58 West Street
Brighton BN1 2RA
UK

Design and layout by Clare Barber

Printed in China

To my family and friends,
and all the other
precious gems in my life.

CONTENTS

Section 3

CRYSTAL SOURCEBOOK 78

INTRODUCTION

This book will take you on a journey. You will discover not only what you truly seek and how to manifest your true desires, but also how to engage in a unique relationship with the magical stones which light up these pages.

My own journey befriending crystals began many years ago, when I was in my twenties. After a series of disastrous love affairs, I thoroughly immersed myself in esoterica, in an attempt to understand and work with my own psychological issues. I knew there was more to the concept of "love" than just physical desire, emotional need, and idealistic fantasies. So, I learned to be mindful and compassionate yet engage fully with life; to conjure spells and divine the moment's energy, and to experience the moment as it is—the eternal now of universal oneness. But where was human love in all this, I wondered. As I sat one day on a cold, English pebbly beach watching the tide come in, the surf flung a few stones close to my hands. One smooth, shining, dark pebble stood out from the other gray ones. Less than two inches (5 cm) long, black and oval, it had a narrow etched line around its circumference, and another line encircling one end. To me it was a sign from the universe, as if this small stone, which had been washed along many shores, raised from the Earth's crust and seen millions of years of evolution, held all of eternity in its matrix. I picked up my new friend and held it in my hand. In those moments I understood the magic of unconditional human love.

However each of us describes it, this kind of feeling can only ever be experienced by oneself to fully understand it, but it felt as if I was truly in touch with the energy of the universe and how it moves through all things, including pebbles, rocks, the swishing tide, and human beings. And so began my relationship with my new friends. Throughout the years, many other crystals have guided me to know not only my true intentions and how to follow my heart, but they have also helped me to manifest goals.

This little black stone still sits on my desk, reminding me that love is all around and that we only need to truly seek it to find it. But doing so with a positive engagement with the universe takes a little wisdom and practice. This book will point you down the right pathway to manifest what you seek and to know what truly matters to you— whether you want to find new love tomorrow, discover career success in just a few months, or simply feel enriched by life everyday. It's time to start the journey and make friends with these very precious stones.

❁ Whether in the ocean, a pebble, a gemstone, or yourself, the energy of the universe permeates all.

HOW TO USE THIS BOOK

Crystals for Positive Manifestation is packed with practical advice and fascinating information about each stone. Not only will you find out about a crystal's attributes, legendary powers, and holistic benefits, you will also gain insight into the unique energy of each stone and how you can use this to manifest your dreams. This book is easy to use and has been divided up into three sections that will carry you on your journey toward positive manifestation.

SECTION ONE

Use this first part of the book to get to know the crystal world and to understand more about how crystals can be used for divination and healing as well as for manifesting your dreams. If you've never worked with crystals before then start at the beginning and enjoy the ride. You will first find out what crystals are made of, where they come from, their scientific heritage, and their historical uses. Discover the basics of working with crystals, their connection to our invisible physical energy centers, known as chakras, and the importance of color in our world. There is information on caring for and choosing crystals, plus a fascinating bit of background on the use of these stones through the ages, which gives an insight into why these particular stones have been used for centuries to help us achieve our goals.

● Enjoy caring for your crystals as if they were your friends and they will bring light into your life.

SECTION TWO

The Manifestation section explains how to use this way of bringing to life the things you desire or truly seek for the future. It gives you practical exercises for learning how to follow your own pathway to achieve your goals. Each step toward manifesting your desire is explained in detail. Don't skip any of the steps, or you may just find yourself back at square one. At the end of the section are four example rituals, using grids and symbols for four different goals. You can try these out to connect you to the magic of the crystals and the magic of yourself.

SECTION THREE

The final section, the Crystal Sourcebook, is divided into four parts: Abundance, Success, Love, and Well-Being. This is to enable you to match your chosen desires with a particular theme. Once you know what your intention is and you have found the relevant crystal section, you can either flick through the pages until you come across a stone that seems to resonate with something deep within you (whether this is because of its color, name, or description) or choose a crystal with its detailed list of attributes in mind. So, for example, if you are looking for new romance, then the Love section will provide you with the most empowering list of crystals. If you can't find the exact crystal you want in stores or online, draw on the associated crystals listed in the entry, or other crystals which attract your attention as you look through the category. By befriending and working with these stones, you will be able to draw on their manifesting powers.

⬤ Manifestation magic will only work if you learn to become a part of it yourself.

⬤ Choose crystals to work with by theme or color, or simply pick one that draws you to it.

The following information is given about each of the 100 crystals:
• Appearance/color
• Current availability
• Physiological correspondences
• Psychological correspondences
• Associated crystals by color
• Keywords

Also included is the crystal's general make-up, where it's most likely to be found, its attributes, its powers, and finally a brief tip on how to use this specific crystal to help you achieve your goal.

So, enjoy the journey and let these magical stones put you on course for happiness, success, love, and abundance.

Section 1:

CRYSTAL BASICS

. . . .

Before you start to use crystals to manifest your dreams, it's important to know how to choose, care for, and program them. You will also need to know about the different types, shapes, and colors available, as well as some of their other uses. This section will give you an insight into all of these fundamental aspects. It will also reveal how crystals are formed, their historical uses, legends, and their powers.

WHAT ARE CRYSTALS?

You may already have a selection of beautiful crystals on your window ledge or wear certain stones as jewelry. Whatever your initial contact, crystals are here to help you connect to and amplify your own powers of manifestation. In fact, your crystal friends will enable you to find whatever you truly seek, whether harmony, well-being, or abundance in your life. Not only are they the treasures of the Earth, they are as much a part of the universe as you are, so treat them with respect. They have ancient heritage and amazing powers. So, how did crystals come into being?

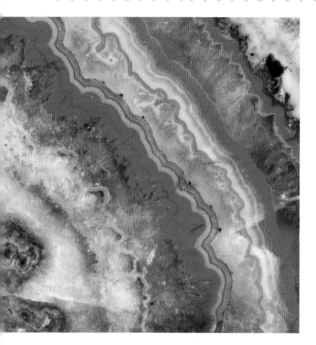

The vivid bands of color found in agate occur from impurities or inclusions of minerals like iron oxide, which creates a variety of reds.

EARTH POWER

The formation of rock, crystal, gems, and other geological strata has been an ongoing process over the course of millions of years. The Earth was once a white-hot, molten ball. Gradually, over eons, a thin layer of this molten ball, known as magma, cooled down to create a crust on the outer surface of the Earth. At the deeper layers of the crust, the molten magma is still a raging furnace, and this permeates the upper strata as volcanic activity or hot springs. Crystals were formed due to these changing temperatures deep within the crust, as well as the fusion of gases, the upheaval of molten material, and the constant stress between the Earth's plates. The absorption of various minerals, such as iron or manganese, gives rise to the many different colors and shapes of crystals. For example, agates are formed from layers of quartz laid in bands. Obsidian was formed by the sudden cooling of molten lava, which meant it had no time to "crystallize" and it is a matte umber color when left unpolished.

ANIMATED STONES

Many ancient peoples believed that everything is alive with a divine, cosmic, or universal energy. This force that flows through all things, whether human being, bird, tree, or plant, also emanates from rocks and stones. So an "alive" yet dormant crystal carries not only powerful Earth energy but also universal energy. Known as *chi* by the ancient Taoists and *mana* in Polynesian culture, and similar to the ancient Greco-Roman concept of *Anima Mundi*—the view that the world is a living being with a soul and intelligence—this invisible force flows through every crystal. That is why crystals are bridges connecting you to the deeper workings of the universe.

VIBRATION

Crystals are alive in another way too. Their vibrational energy, known as the piezoelectric effect, was discovered by French physicist and chemist, Pierre Curie (1859–1906). In simple terms, when mechanical stress is applied to a crystal—for instance, by squeezing it—a voltage is produced across the crystal's surface.

In fact, try it now yourself. Hold a crystal tightly in your hand and you will feel it warm up. What you are doing is applying stress to the crystal so that its electromagnetic force comes alive. This effect is reversible and if the polarity of the voltage is alternated, the crystal will rapidly expand and contract, producing a vibration—warm to cool, cool to warm, warm to cool, and so on. This is how quartz watches work.

By learning to use our own magical power of attraction, we can harness these vibrational forces and help ourselves manifest our dreams. For example, we can resonate to the low vibrational field of obsidian to manifest a reliable, consistent home life. Or we can arrange a selection of high-resonance citrine in a grid to attract abundance.

● Quartz watches are a notable example of the piezoelectric effect in action. The quartz crystal within the mechanism produces its own electromagnetic force to keep the watch ticking over.

So, in this book we're going to discover 100 essential living crystals that will help you manifest your dreams, desires, and goals. By letting these stones into your life, nurturing them, and respecting their powers, you can cross that other bridge—the one that leads to a better quality of life or to the fulfillment of your desires. You can finally discover what you truly seek; but first you need to know what that is (see page 52).

CRYSTALS in HISTORY and LEGEND

Over six thousand years ago, the ancient Babylonians believed that crystals were placed on Earth as gifts from the planetary gods they worshipped. These artful people were also great magicians and astrologers. They used crystals in their magic formulas and spells, and even used them to predict the future, believing each stone was filled with cosmic or divine energy. The ancient scribes of the Old Testament noted that Noah's Ark was thought to be illuminated by one precious garnet, while later medieval crusaders wore garnets as amulets to protect them against attack.

ANCIENT EGYPT

In ancient Egypt, gemstones were used not only for magic rituals, but also to improve health and for cosmetic purposes. Lapis lazuli was revered for its exquisite blue color, which symbolized the heavens, and was used for decorating funeral masks, such as that of Pharaoh Tutankhamun (ca. 1341–1323 BCE). To the Egyptians, jasper represented fire, life, and blood, while malachite represented new growth and fertility. It has even been speculated that the pyramids were capped with crystals to channel cosmic forces down through the geometric structures. To reveal their powerful rank, Egyptian master builders wore carnelian, thought to be the stone of form and design. The 29th chapter of the ancient Egyptain funerary text, the *Book of the Dead*, was inscribed on a carnelian stone and many carnelian amulets were placed in the coffins of the departed. These were engraved with messages for Isis and other gods to ensure safe passage of the body to the afterlife. Later, in the Middle Ages, alchemists used carnelian as a boiling stone to activate the energy of other crystals used in spells and recipes.

Tutankhamun's funeral mask uses crystals for protection in the afterlife.

ANTIQUITY

The ancient Greeks believed that every piece of clear quartz crystal was water frozen by the gods, and called it *crystallos*, meaning "icicle." Roman ladies carried it during the summer to keep their hands cool, while opals, associated with Hermes, the god of trade and travel in Greek mythology, were used to attract fortune and good trade. To the Greeks, wearing an agate ring meant you would be favored by the gods, while according to the Roman historian and writer Pliny, the Persian magi burnished agate stones to avert storms. The magicians proved the crystal's power by throwing agate into a cauldron of boiling water, which would miraculously cool down.

POWER STONES

Emeralds were sold in the markets of Babylon as early as 4,000 BCE and the ancient Chaldeans believed each stone contained the essence of the goddess Ishtar. The ancient Egyptians believed emeralds were a gift from Thoth, the god of wisdom. Rediscovered a hundred years ago in Egypt are ancient emerald mines thought to be some of the oldest in the world. They are known as Cleopatra's Mines, after the ancient queen's love of the stone. Emeralds were also talismans of Aristotle, Alexander the Great, Charlemagne, and the moguls of India. Another greenish stone, aventurine, was used by Tibetan monks for the eyes of statues, to reveal the god's visionary power. Wearing aventurine was also believed to improve sight and enhance spiritual power.

● Emeralds were often used as a magical aid to call up spirits and propitiate the gods in ancient Mesopotamia.

● It was once believed that emeralds contained the essence of the ancient Sumerian goddess Ishtar.

Statues, jars, vases, and jewelry made of jade date back thousands of years. The ancient Chinese thought the stone would bring the user wealth and happiness.

Jade is revered as a noble stone throughout Asia. Among its many attributes are its association with the sun and its powerful yang energy. It was also believed to be a panacea, or remedy for all diseases, in ancient China. Jade carved in the shape of a butterfly still has a special significance for engaged couples. A legend tells of a how a young man, in pursuit of a butterfly, ventured into a private garden of a rich lord. Instead of being punished for his trespass, he ended up marrying the lord's daughter. A symbol of happily-ever-after romance, bridegrooms often give their fiancées a jade butterfly to ensure a good marriage.

PROTECTIVE STONES

Peridot has been used both as protection against evil and a crystal of change. This olive-green stone was used by ancient civilizations as a charm to ward off sorcery, evil spirits, and madness. It was usually set in gold and worn as jewelry. In more recent times, in the ninth century, the Archbishop of Mainz, Rabanus Maurus, believed peridot was one of the 12 apocalyptic gems reflecting spiritual truths. In the 16th century, the astrologer and magician Cornelius Agrippa declared that peridot held to the sun would soothe the respiratory system and heal asthma. Throughout the European medieval period, peridot was ground down into powder and sold in apothecary stores as an antidote for madness and nightmares.

In Roman times, peridot was thought to bestow its wearer with the power of the great emperors.

MAGICAL STONES

Another legendary crystal is the multicolored opal. Ancient Aboriginal Australians believed that when the Creator came down to Earth on a rainbow, at the very spot where his foot touched the ground the stones came alive. Sparkling with all the colors of the rainbow, they became the stones we know as opals. Another Aboriginal legend tells of a gigantic opal-like Creator, who ruled the stars, love, and gold mines.

The Roman historian and author Pliny described the opal as a stone containing all at once "the garnet's fiery flame, the amethyst's resplendent purple, and the emerald's sea-green glory." The most mysterious of gems to the ancient Greeks, it was worn to strengthen the sight, heal diseases of the eyes, and to invoke great luck. But despite ancient belief that it contained the essence of all the most important gemstones, it fell from grace in the nineteenth century when it became linked with misfortune. Opal was redeemed in the twentieth century and is today firmly back in favor.

Pyrite, also more commonly known as "fool's gold" was considered a stone of power and great magic, frequently used by indigenous North American shamans. They carved pyrite into amulets and used natural stones for divination or for healing ceremonies and magical spells. Both the Incas of Peru and the Mexican Aztecs polished large slabs or impressive pieces of pyrite into mirrors for fortune telling and scrying. While one side was usually polished flat, the other was highly convex and frequently carved with special symbolic markings to invoke spirits and oracular messages.

● Many stones appear to glitter or have a luminescent quality—none more so than opals, which were once thought to encapsulate the power of all known crystals.

CRYSTAL USAGE

We've seen how crystals have been used for centuries as decorations, talismans, or amulets, as well as for magic, divination, healing, protection, and attracting positive energy or manifesting dreams. Nothing much has changed, except these days we have access to a larger choice of stones than ever and many more people around the world are becoming aware of the power of crystals. So, let's have a look at what you can use your beautiful stones for, aside from manifesting your dreams.

PROTECTION

Due to the electromagnetic energy exuded and absorbed by crystals, many can be used to protect you from the negative psychic energy of others or simply from geopathic stress around you. The Earth has a natural energy field and geopathic stress occurs when something disturbs this flow of energy, either above or beneath the Earth's surface. This can be anything from a diverted water course under your house, electric pylons near your home, or blocked ley lines, to springs and electric cables beneath your feet, underground trains, and fissures in nearby rocks. Crystals such as black tourmaline, obsidian, and smoky quartz can be placed in the home to absorb negative energy. (See page 74 for information on manifesting a harmonious home.)

Wearing amber beads is perfect protection from negative energy and will bring you tranquility.

You can also wear or carry crystals to protect you from the negative energy of others. For example, you may have envious colleagues or neighbors, a difficult partner, or experience discomfort in a crowd. Wearing amber will protect you from the toxic or polluted thoughts of others, while carrying fluorite will guard you from general geopathic stress in the environment.

HEALING

Using crystals to heal a medical or physical condition requires training, practice, or the consultation of a qualified therapist. Crystals can be placed on various points around the body to calm or energize physical symptoms, but it is only advisable to do this after seeking professional advice.

Crystal healing is holistic and can be used to realign our energy so that we are healed emotionally, spiritually, and physically. For spiritual healing, where we need to reconnect to our soul or the universe, or simply gain a renewed sense of our spiritual self, we can meditate with certain crystals, such as amethyst, celestite, or moonstone. But for emotional and spiritual healing, you can use a range of crystals to boost your well-being, balance your chakra energies, and enhance your emotions and general psychological state. For instance, red garnet balances sexual energy levels and alleviates emotional disharmony, while brown jasper stimulates the immune system.

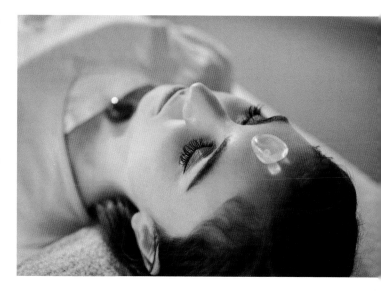

Placing crystals, such as moonstone, in alignment with your chakras is one way to begin holistic healing, but it should be done under professional guidance.

DIVINATION

Like many forms of magic and divination, crystals correspond to symbolic languages such as astrology, tarot, runes, and feng shui. Because crystals' vibrational power connects them to the universe, they can be used as a conduit or channel for cosmic knowledge from the past, present, and future. This means you can "divine" the future by placing crystals in special layouts or grids. We will be using grids to create magic symbols for manifestation purposes later in this book. Some crystals correspond or vibrate to the resonance of the planets and can be laid out in various geometrical designs to capture the essence of a certain symbol. These can then be interpreted as oracles, or can be taken from a pouch and used as a crystal guide for the day ahead. You can also use a dowsing crystal to help you find lost objects or make important decisions for the future.

MAGIC

In a way, magic is like manifestation, in that we are making things happen. So although crystals are often used in magic spells and rituals, placed on altars, or in sacred places, they are in fact doing the same job as when we want something to happen as if by magic. Crystals connect the magic part of ourselves to the magic of the universe.

CRYSTAL SHAPES

Crystals come in all shapes and sizes and many are now artificially "formed" to create attractive structures that enhance their energy. Here are the most common crystal shapes. This list should help you decide which ones to use. Although natural and terminated are the most popular shapes for manifestation purposes, there are many others which work their magic just as powerfully.

NATURAL

Most crystals are just little pieces of rock. Some are left in their natural state but often they are polished, to create "tumbled" stones. Many people are drawn to natural-looking shapes because they show the true matrix of the crystal's formation. Carry these stones with you, place them in grids, or position them in specific parts of the home.

TERMINATED

Terminated crystals have pointed ends and are powerful tools for manifestation. Single-terminated crystals can remove negative energy or attract power, depending on whether you point them toward or away from you. With double-terminated crystals energy is drawn in and output simultaneously. Terminated crystals can be used alone or to amplify the manifestation power of other crystals in a grid.

SINGLE-TERMINATED

DOUBLE-TERMINATED

GEODE

Geodes are usually small, cavern-like formations or rock lined with crystals. The geode's shape collects, stores, and then amplifies the crystal's power. These are useful structures for creating abundance and are usually placed on an altar, shelf, or table to act as a "generator" crystal for other manifestation work.

CLUSTER

These are usually clusters of crystal ridges and points, which stem out in different directions from a main center. They beam energy all over the surrounding area and are great to place in the home to manifest harmony and peace.

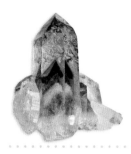

PHANTOM

Often pyramid-shaped and laid down in many layers, phantom crystals are usually quartz and generally used for spiritual and healing work. But placed on an altar or sacred space, they may be used to help clarify what your deepest self truly seeks.

BALL

Famous as tools for clairvoyants, crystal balls are artificially formed spheres that emit power in every possible direction. They reflect their user's desires and are often used as an oracular tool for "scrying" (reading the future).

FLAT

Many crystals resemble flat stones you might find on a beach and are often about the size you can hold comfortably in the palm of one hand. These are great for carrying around with you. Held in your hand, a crystal suited to your particular goal will help you to focus your intention and manifest your desire.

MANIFESTATION

Manifestation crystals are man-made structures formed by encasing a smaller crystal in a larger one of the same type. They are often placed in the center of a manifestation grid to amplify their power.

BED

A bed of many smaller pieces of crystal spread across a solid crystal base acts as a powerful attractive force. It is useful to place a crystal bed on an altar or in the home, so that it emanates a continuous source of energy.

SCEPTER

Similar to an ornamental staff or a magician's wand, the scepter usually has a central rod with a larger portion of the crystal extending around it at one end. This shape is often used to reclaim power or to activate pure intention before you begin to use other crystals for manifestation.

CRYSTAL COLORS

We all have our favorite colors. This often changes with time and in psychological or spiritual circles our choice of favorite and least-favorite colors is determined by our state of mind or emotions. We are attracted to a color sometimes because we "need" more of what that color represents in our life. Alternatively, we might be attracted to a color because we are filled with the quality that color embodies. The colors we don't like are often symbolic of something inside our psychological makeup that we haven't addressed. For example, we may hate the color red and its correspondence to passion because that's actually the very thing we lack in our lives and we are denying our need for a vibrant love life. So we can use specific crystals to enhance our best qualities or to attract what we need or seek into our life.

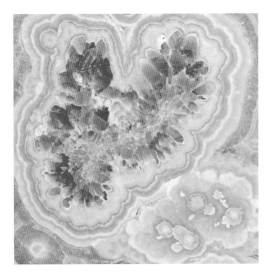

For the purposes of manifestation, color is just as important as shape or symbol. In fact, when you think about it, you know that red is linked to passion, yellow to vibrancy, purple to wisdom, and pink to romance. We are already unconsciously aware of these correspondences, so if you wanted to attract love and manifest a passionate romance, it might already be pretty obvious that you would work with both pink and red crystals to get results.

⬤ The color pink's ancient correspondence with romance and love is embedded in our psyche.

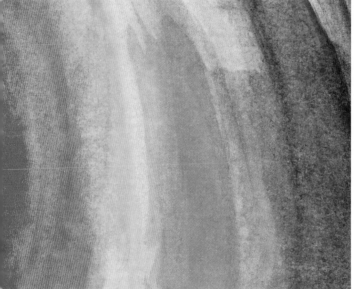

COLOR VIBRATIONS

The vibrations of crystals correspond to the color spectrum, or invisible waves of energy. This spectrum includes radio waves and various types of ray—infrared, ultraviolet, visible light, X-rays, and gamma rays. In the visible part of this spectrum, the colors we humans can see range from the low-frequency vibration of the color red, to the shortest wavelength and highest frequency, ultraviolet. The electromagnetic vibration of crystal energy also corresponds to this color spectrum.

Looking at a rainbow, we only see the major colors. These colors (including many tonal variations) are those associated with crystals.

So which colors do you prefer in your life at the moment? The general rule is that if a color makes you feel good about yourself, carrying or wearing a crystal of that color will enhance its special qualities within you.

Knowing what the different colors mean and the energy they invoke in your life means you can easily understand the basics of crystal power. For the purposes of manifestation, the following pages provide a quick rundown of the colors and how they can generally help you.

CRYSTAL COLOR GUIDE

Use the following guide to to help you decide which color of stone to use to manifest your desires. For example, if you are seeking career success, you would be advised to pick green. Then, just look through the green stone list to see the most common crystals for manifesting your intention.

BLUE

Blue has long been thought to enhance intuition, generate compassion, and invoke spiritual development. Blue crystals include violet and lavender varieties of agate and tourmaline. Blue helps to manifest our true intentions by fine-tuning our intuitive powers. For example, celestite would help you to trust the signs or pathway set before you so that you could be confident in knowing what it is you desire.

SAPPHIRE: *Wisdom, prosperity*

BLUE LACE AGATE: *Clarity, focus, peace*

LAPIS LAZULI: *Truth*

AQUAMARINE: *Intuition, foresight*

BLUE TOPAZ: *Trust, attainment of goals*

BLUE AGATE

RED

Red is the color of passion, growth, impulse, power, action, courage, and love. Red signifies fire but also blood, the life force and the energy that gets us moving. Red empowers, uplifts, and gets things done. Red is all about action and drive. Red jasper, for example, is a great choice for amplifying your intention and to manifest any creative process. Other red crystals, such as carnelian, garnet, and ruby, help to free you from being indecisive and manifest passion in your life.

BLOODSTONE: *Empowerment, determination*

RUBY: *Passion, potency*

GARNET: *Willpower, charisma*

RED CARNELIAN: *Endurance, motivation, success*

RED JASPER: *Success, results, achievement*

GOLDSTONE (MAN-MADE REDDISH STONE): *Prosperity, wealth*

RED JASPER

YELLOW/ORANGE

Yellow is thought to be the color of wisdom, joy, and happiness. It is also the color that brings clarity, abundance, a sharp mind, and focused intention. Known as the ultimate stone of abundance, citrine is renowned for its ability to attract what you most desire— similarly, cinnabar attracts richness of mind, emotions, and material wealth.

CITRINE: *Abundance, reward, optimism*

AMBER: *Joy, comfort, well-being*

YELLOW TOPAZ: *Decision-making, clarity*

YELLOW FLUORITE: *Quick thinking, ideas*

ORANGE CALCITE: *Intellectual power*

SUNSTONE: *Opportunity, inner wealth, outer wealth*

CITRINE

GREEN

Green is the color of self-respect, well-being, and balance. It also symbolizes growth harmony, and can enhance material and financial success or bring money to you. Green jade is a useful stone for manifesting successful business and wealth. All green crystals have the power to bring change, or help you to pursue new ideas or free yourself from the demands of others.

MALACHITE: *Material abundance, change*

GREEN TOURMALINE: *Success, money*

JADE: *Financial reward, decision-making*

EMERALD: *Wisdom, inspiration, inner richness*

PERIDOT: *Clarity, opportunity*

GREEN AVENTURINE: *Prosperity, leadership*

MALACHITE

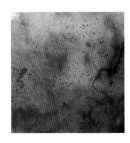

BLACK/BROWN

Although black is not technically a color because it absorbs all light, black stones are key crystals for manifestation. Black gemstones symbolize self-control and resilience, while brown aligns with the material side of life. Stones such as obsidian help us to attract stability and down-to-earth rewards, while black moonstone, for instance, will attract mentors.

BLACK TOURMALINE: *Home harmony, grounding*

ONYX: *Strength, self-control, potential*

JET: *Harmony, protection, balance*

MAHOGANY OBSIDIAN: *Self-belief, awareness, empowerment*

OBSIDIAN: *Self-confidence, material gain*

MAGNETITE: *Endurance, tenacity*

MAHOGANY OBSIDIAN

WHITE/CLEAR/PINK

White or clear crystals are symbolic of new beginnings. White or clear quartz clears clutter and obstacles away, brings mental and spiritual clarity, and purifies thoughts and actions so you can see how to truly be fortunate. Clear quartz is a brilliant "generator" crystal to use with grids for amplifying intentions. Pink crystals invoke feelings of caring, tenderness, self-worth, love, and acceptance, so rose quartz and rhodochrosite manifest love and romance.

MOONSTONE: *New beginnings, spiritual clarity*

CLEAR QUARTZ: *Amplifies desire, clarity, generates success*

WHITE SELENITE: *Peace, compassion, love*

WHITE TOPAZ: *Truth, clarity, peace of mind*

ROSE QUARTZ: *New love, romance, harmony*

RHODOCHROSITE: *Self-worth, value, acceptance*

RHODOCHROSITE

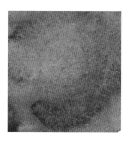

PURPLE/VIOLET

Purple and violet have long been used to symbolize magic, mystery, and spirituality, and were once a color favored by royalty. Amethyst, a mixture of red—dynamic and active energy—and blue—otherworldly and intuitive—can be used to manifest creative ideas, access one's imagination and inspiration, and invite pure universal wisdom.

AMETHYST: *Spiritual wisdom, intuition, serenity*

PURPLE SAPPHIRE: *Awakening, truth, awareness*

PURPLE FLUORITE: *Psychic power, deeper knowledge*

SUGILITE: *Self-understanding, revelation*

CHAROITE: *Transformation, unconditional love*

AMETHYST

CHOOSING CRYSTALS

Some of us make choices impulsively and spontaneously. We don't always reflect or weigh up the value of each possible outcome. These "choices" are sometimes those that later we describe as coming from the heart—from intuition or instinct. That's why, when you choose a crystal, you are more likely to react personally to its color, shape, or look, rather than a calculated or logical reason for acquiring it. However, when choosing crystals for manifesting your dreams, you require a little knowledge about which crystals can help you achieve your intended goal and which may be better used for another purpose. So, before you start to choose crystals, be sure you know what it is that you seek. More on that on page 52.

When you pick out a crystal in a store, the chances are that the crystal has picked you out too!

ATTRACTION FACTOR

You know how you can be drawn to someone across a crowded room, and they to you? Well, the same goes for your attraction to a crystal. These stones are saying something to you; they are living stones and their essence resonates with your current state of being, perhaps because you lack the qualities that the crystal embodies or you desire that quality in yourself. Never underestimate your reasons for choosing a crystal, and afterward, apart from cleansing and programming it, always thank it for being there and finding you.

SOURCING

Sourcing crystals is easy these days thanks to the Internet. Although you can buy them directly online, personally I always go to a specialty store where I can touch, see, and hold the crystal in my hand. It is important to attune to your crystal's energy and sometimes you will find a crystal "calls" you to hold it—a sign that you are right to take it and make it a friend in your life right now.

When you are browsing, hold each crystal in your hand until you know it's the right one for you. Take your time—this can take thirty seconds for each stone. Sometimes you will feel a vibrational energy or have an intuitive flash. This is a sign that you're in tune with the energy of the crystal and its connection to cosmic power. After you have chosen your crystal and it is in your possession, repeat the following: "My crystal friend, thank you for finding me."

ZODIAC CHOICE

Crystals correspond to the twelve signs of the zodiac and there are many diverse lists of stones and crystals associated with the signs. Some say the crystal is associated with the month rather than the zodiac. Whatever the case, here is my personal preferred list according to the symbol, color, and correspondences with astrological lore. Note that when you choose a crystal because of its affinity with your sun sign, it can also be used as a generator stone for any of the manifestation grids described in Section 2.

To help you understand what you truly seek, and to enhance your own sun-sign qualities, wear your crystal as jewelry or carry a piece in a pouch or bag.

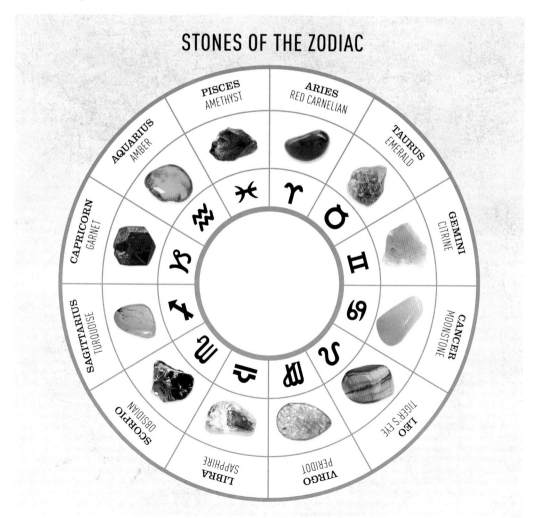

STONES OF THE ZODIAC

PISCES — AMETHYST
ARIES — RED CARNELIAN
AQUARIUS — AMBER
TAURUS — EMERALD
CAPRICORN — GARNET
GEMINI — CITRINE
SAGITTARIUS — TURQUOISE
CANCER — MOONSTONE
SCORPIO — OBSIDIAN
LEO — TIGER'S EYE
LIBRA — SAPPHIRE
VIRGO — PERIDOT

CARING *for* CRYSTALS

Many crystals become dust collectors simply because we leave them lying around on ledges and forget them. Please don't do this as they won't ever help you to manifest anything, except more dust! (Do you leave your friends to sit on a ledge and get dusty?) Remember to talk to them as you would your best friend. Also touch them, handle them, or take them out with you when you go somewhere special.

Dedicate a special sacred place for your crystals, keep them safely in a pouch and carry this around with you, arrange them on a desk where you can handle them frequently, or simply wear them as jewelry. It may just be one crystal you're tuning in to, so that you can manifest something specific, but you should *still* make sure you care for this crystal as you would your best friend.

● The ritual of washing crystals cleanses them of negative energy picked up on their journey to you.

Most crystals, apart from polished "tumbled" stones, will need to be wrapped in a silk or cotton scarf or cloth to prevent scratching, unless you are placing them at various points in the home. Always cleanse crystals after purchase, particularly jewelry that may have been worn by someone else and may still carry their psychic footprints.

CLEANSING

When you first bring your crystal home, if you are lucky enough to live by the sea or a stream, gently immerse the stone in the ocean or under the fresh running water— or if you don't have access to either, under a tap. As you do so, affirm in your mind or out loud that all negativity will be washed away and positive energy will permeate the crystal.

You can also leave the crystal on a window ledge for three days and nights in a row to recharge its energy in natural light.

FIRE, EARTH, AIR, AND WATER RITUAL

 Another way to cleanse and re-energize your crystals is by using this ritual. The energy of the four elements brings the crystal into harmony with your wishes and desires.

WHAT YOU WILL NEED:

- Your crystal(s)
- A white candle
- A bowl of spring water
- A piece of paper and pen

WHAT TO DO:

1 Write down the name or names of your new crystals on the piece of paper in a list (they can be in any order) and place the stones alongside their names. This action represents the element of Air, which is associated with naming things. Words are magical and as soon as we invoke the crystal by naming it aloud, we are bringing it to life in our own world.

2 Now gaze at the crystals on your paper and try to visualize them surrounded by golden light from the core of the Earth, cleansing, energizing, and nurturing them. As you gaze at them, name them one by one, repeating their names again and again at least ten times. This is the Earth ritual.

3 Now light the candle, and take each crystal in turn and pass it slowly through the top of the candle flame—being careful not to burn yourself. This is how you cleanse and energize a stone by Fire.

4 Next, for the Water ritual, place the crystals on the table in a circle next to the bowl of water. If you have only one or two crystals, place them in the center of the table. Touch each stone in turn with a drop of water on your finger. As you do so, say the following for each crystal:

Crystal friend, you are now cleansed and purified.

5 Finally, thank the crystals for being there for you and then blow out the candle. Your crystals are now ready to be dedicated and/or programmed.

DEDICATING YOUR CRYSTALS

Once you have your crystals in your possession, you need to dedicate them with the intention that only positive energy will flow through them and that they are only going to be used for the good of all. This dedication will also focus all the goodness of the universe into the crystals and prevents the stones from retaining any negative energy—whether they have acquired this from the handling of others or from geopathic stress deep within the Earth's surface.

Crystals are very receptive to our blessings. Their energy must be respected and honored, using specific rituals.

Although crystals absorb and neutralize negative energy, turning it into positive energy, outside influences can linger if the stone hasn't been used or treated with love or care for some time. Many stones are handled by lots of people before they even get to a store, and if you have bought one on the Internet, you will also have the energy of the crystal's journey before it reaches your own hands. It's important to dedicate your crystals to positive healing energies to protect them from negative influences in the future, too.

DEDICATION RITUAL

WHAT TO DO:

1 Sit down in a quiet place with the crystal cupped in your hands. Close your eyes and focus on your breathing, taking deep, slow, regular breaths.

2 Imagine that beneath your feet is a golden casket, and within the casket are all the crystals you will ever need to help you fulfill your desires. As you concentrate on the casket, imagine a golden light radiating from the casket and rising up through you, until it fills every pore of your body. As the light spreads through you it enters the crystal in your hand, filling it with all the powers of all the other crystals in the golden casket.

3 Now visualize a ray of pure white light beaming down from above, as if it has come from the galaxies and the universe. As this light envelops you it merges with the golden light, so the crystal is both protected and filled with positive energy.

4 Either say aloud or in your mind:

This crystal is dedicated to the highest good and for the power of manifesting my dream.

5 Now open your eyes and gaze at your stone while repeating the dedication to the crystal five times and ending with:

So will it be.

You can also dedicate your stone to a specific entity that protects and guides you, such as a deity, saint, guardian angel, or spirit guide. Once you have completed your dedication, you will find yourself more in tune with your crystal's powers and ready to program it.

PROGRAMMING *your* CRYSTALS *for* MANIFESTATION

A crystal can be programmed so that its energy is focused on something specific, meaning your intention is reinforced by the crystal's own power. Once a stone has been programmed, it will continually work with that desire until it is cleared or reprogrammed. Although one crystal can enhance various intentions, it is important not to use the wrong crystal either. In other words, don't program a crystal (let's say, rose quartz) for success in a career, when actually it is better employed for manifesting love.

REFINING YOUR INTENTIONS

So, how do you know what your intentions are? Turn to page 56 to discover more about focused intention before doing this exercise.

Once you know what it is you seek, make sure you also have your best intentions for the crystal. Be specific about your desire and precise with your thoughts or words—don't waffle! If you want to find a new career or job, describe exactly what kind of work you are seeking.

Blue stones help us to trust in our intuition and feel confident about the manifestation process.

Select a stone that resonates with your desire. Use the different sections of this book to check which category the stone may be best used for. Make sure it is the right type of crystal for your purpose. For example, if you are looking for a peaceful home life, choose a crystal that is already used for calmness and serenity, such as selenite. If you want an energizing stone to stimulate action or to bring positive results quickly, red stones, such as red carnelian or red jasper, will work well. If you seek greater communication between yourself and work colleagues, chose a yellow stone such as citrine.

PROGRAMMING RITUAL

WHAT TO DO:

1 Sit quietly with your crystal in the palm of your hand and think about your desire. Keep repeating this desire or intention over and over, aloud or in your head.

2 Gaze at the crystal and relax, feeling in harmony with the energy of the crystal. Now repeat your desire several times out loud to fix it to the crystal, so it has absorbed all of your intention.

3 Once a stone has been programmed, depending on its purpose, wear the stone, carry it in your pocket, or place it by your bed. It can also be beneficial to hold the crystal and repeat your intention several times a day.

4 Keep any specifically programmed crystals out of contact with others to avoid them being affected by other energies and vibrations, which may disturb your own programming. Protect the crystal by wrapping it in silk or cotton when not in use.

DEPROGRAMMING

If you decide you no longer have this particular desire, or it has been fulfilled, to deprogram a crystal simply sit comfortably with the stone in your hand and say:

All that I desired is no longer my intention. Crystal, be as you once were.

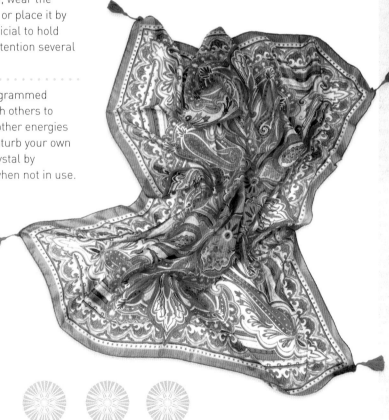

CRYSTALS and the CHACKRAS

Crystals are often used to restore balance to the chakras (a Sanskrit word, meaning "wheels"). The chakras are epicenters of invisible energy believed to flow around and through the body. Likened to whirlwinds or spirals of air that vibrate at different frequencies, they form an invisible interface connecting our personal body energy and the chi, or cosmic energy, which flows through all things. The chakras also correspond to the energy of seven colors, which are traditionally associated with seven gemstones (see the illustration on the opposite page).

By wearing specific gemstones for each chakra, you can increase your energy levels and enhance your manifestation powers. The chakra colors are red, orange, yellow, green, blue, indigo, and violet. If the chakras are not balanced, or if the energies are blocked, you may find you have negative thoughts or become physically tired or depressed. When the chakras are functioning normally, each will automatically respond to the particular energies needed from the universal energy field.

On the following illustration you can see the position of the seven major chakras, but for manifestation purposes we need to know that there are two other important energy centers. These two chakras are concerned with "giving out" to the universe but also with receiving from the universe. Quite simply, these energy centers lie in the palms of your hands.

Aligning specific crystals with the chakras brings about harmony and well-being, and a sense of what truly matters to you.

THE NINE CHAKRAS

6. THE THIRD EYE CHAKRA
Located in the center of the brow, the third eye vibrates to the color indigo and is concerned with inspiration, imagination, and psychic ability.

7. THE CROWN CHAKRA
Situated on the top of the head, this is the center for true spirituality and enlightenment. It allows for the inward flow of wisdom and brings the gift of cosmic consciousness.

4. THE HEART CHAKRA
Situated behind the breastbone and in front of the spine, the heart chakra vibrates to the colors green and pink, and is the center of warm, loving feelings. This chakra is about true compassion, love, and spirituality.

5. THE THROAT CHAKRA
The throat chakra is located in the lower end of the throat and is the center for thought, communication, music, speech, and writing.

3. THE SOLAR PLEXUS CHAKRA
Situated between the navel and the breastbone, the third chakra is the seat of personal power. Rather like having one's own inner "sun", it gives us a strong ego, a sense of our own personal character, individuality, and willpower.

2 .THE SACRAL CHAKRA
Located approximately a hand's breadth below the navel, the sacral chakra is concerned with our sex drive, creativity, and emotional state.

1. THE BASE OR ROOT CHAKRA
The base chakra is located at the base of the spine. This chakra is concerned with our sense of being "grounded."

8. and 9. PALM CHAKRAS
In the center of each palm are the chakras for "exchanging" energy. Here we give and receive, offer and accept, and so on. Here we hold crystals to empower us and connect us to the universal energy flow.

GETTING IN TOUCH WITH YOUR PALM CHAKRAS

Follow this exercise to really get in touch with your palm chakras and learn how to connect to the power of a white quartz crystal.

WHAT YOU WILL NEED:

- A white quartz crystal (small enough to hold in your hand)
- A white candle

WHAT TO DO:

1 Place the white quartz on a table and position your candle behind the crystal. Sit comfortably at the table and light the candle. Once the flame becomes more still, take up the white quartz crystal and place it in the palm of your writing hand. Close your eyes and breathe slowly and gently, counting down your breaths from twenty to one, to settle yourself into a calm state.

2 As you let the crystal rest in your palm, notice first what it feels like. Is it cold, warm, soft, hard, heavy, light? Can you feel its energy? Can you sense the power flowing through your palm chakra? Stretch your arm out to one side, as if offering the crystal to the universe and say:

With this crystal, I open my power to manifest to you, the universe.

3 Take the crystal in your other hand and again take note of what it makes you feel. Then repeat the same affirmation and stretch your arm out, as if in offering, on your other side.

4 Next, hold the crystal between both your palms, just in front of your belly button, and gaze on the light and colors that may be refracted within its inner world. Imagine yourself exploring the innermost world of your white quartz crystal until you are reaching the pure light of the universe. Can you sense it is alive? Can you hear what it is telling you?

5 Place the crystal back on the table and repeat the affirmation:

I am blessed by the presence of this crystal and I am empowered by the energy that flows through the universe.

6 Finally, blow or snuff out the candle and gently come back to a normal state. You have now had your first experience of crystal power and your ability to manifest through its connection to the universe. But what exactly is manifestation and how do we successfully do it? Let's find out in the next section.

White or clear quartz crystal is the most empowering and majestic of stones, and can transform your life with a daily touch of the hand.

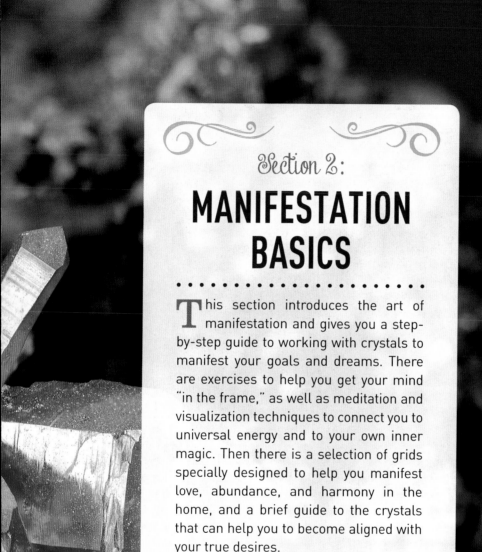

Section 2:

MANIFESTATION BASICS

This section introduces the art of manifestation and gives you a step-by-step guide to working with crystals to manifest your goals and dreams. There are exercises to help you get your mind "in the frame," as well as meditation and visualization techniques to connect you to universal energy and to your own inner magic. Then there is a selection of grids specially designed to help you manifest love, abundance, and harmony in the home, and a brief guide to the crystals that can help you to become aligned with your true desires.

WHAT IS MANIFESTATION?

We all want to make our dreams come true or just make something specific happen. We wish on stars, throw coins in a fountain, believe in luck or fate. But most of us never really empower ourselves with the very essence of manifestation—being at one with not only ourselves, but also the universe within us. The great news is that with the help of your crystal friends you can start to find this sense of oneness and manifest your dreams and goals. Be warned, it takes willingness, intention, goodness, gratitude, effort, passion, and, most of all, self-belief. Manifestation is about letting the universe within you reveal itself through you and your unique identity and desires. But to manifest your dreams you have to really know yourself and what you truly want, or rather what you actually seek. And with that knowledge, you must know how to call on the universal energy within you to make your life complete.

● Tossing coins into fountains is one way to attract happiness, but you must truly believe in your dreams to manifest them.

MANIFESTATION

The word "manifest" derives from the Latin word *manifestus*, meaning clear, apparent, or proved by direct evidence. In other words, whether you have a dream of an abundant lifestyle, a yearning for a house in the country, or a wish for a happy family, you have to make it "real."

We can only make these dreams come true (or bring them into tangible reality) if we are ready to cast off expectations, conditions, assumptions, and emotional poisons—to cut to the core and reveal our true self. This self is the one that lies deep within us, profoundly linked to our soul's purpose and its connection to the universe. In fact, the universe lies within us, just as it appears to lie without us. It is only once we start to really believe this, and by "believe," I mean "know and experience" this, that can we actually manifest that which we desire.

WANTS AND NEEDS

Wanting and needing are two very different things. "Want" implies a lack. When we are "wanting" it is because we don't have whatever it is we think we lack. We feel a sense of missing out—or we feel inadequate in some way because we don't "own" this thing, or quality of life. We may be envious of others who are wealthy or in happy marriages, and so we feel we deserve those things and ought to have them in our own lives. But whether the things we want on the surface are in tandem with what our soul or deeper purpose has intended for us is another matter. This is not about "fate," it is about innate potential and what we truly seek. This is when we have to learn to accept every piece of goodness that we do get, and also learn to let go and trust in the flow of the universe, letting goodness come to us.

When we feel we need a change of scenery, new shoes, or to be loved, we are also expressing a sense of lack. But this time it is about necessity—in other words it is necessary for us to have that thing to make us feel at one with ourselves. It seems essential to our very existence. But, as with wanting, we have to be careful we aren't getting carried away with cultural or family expectations about what we need. Both "want" and "need" are feelings we attach ourselves to throughout life. It is only when we give and receive with no emotional investment— only emotional involvement, enjoying the giving or accepting, observing or being aware of our reactions—that we can really manifest that which we are truly blessed to have.

⬤ A joyful life is one where you are not dependent on other people's expectations or lifestyles. Find what truly matters to you.

THE SEEKER

A seeker is someone who knows that they are looking for something, and are taking responsibility for the quest they are on. The seeker is in everyone, but only some of us are aware there is a questing side to our natures. Some of us repress or deny the seeker, because we fear we will be a failure if we don't get what we seek. That is when the wanting, or needing, egocentric bit of ourselves takes over from the free spirit of the seeker.

Obviously then the seeker in you must first find out what it is you truly seek. Let's take a look at the root of the word. Generally, "to seek" means "to look for," "to desire," or "to wish for." I'm seeking a new career, I'm seeking a pot of gold, I'm seeking enlightenment. But the ancient Indo-European word from which it derives, *sag*, also means "to perceive with wisdom." So, with wise thought, self-understanding, and objective observation, we can learn to seek what is right for us. The seeker in us then becomes aware of what has to manifest, rather than what the ego wants to manifest.

Do you see the sun rising or setting? Rather like the analogy of the half-empty or half-full glass, you can learn a lot about how you perceive the world. This will have an important effect on its responses to your requests.

DO I DESERVE WHAT I SEEK?

Of course, we may think "Do I deserve the best? Do I deserve to be wealthy, or wise, or both? Do I deserve love?" Well, yes you do, just by being a human being on this Earth. And manifesting the things you truly seek is deserved, too.

So, we long to fulfill our goals and dreams, and once we have learned to find our own magic and power—once we have shrugged off the heavy cloak of cultural or family expectations—we are then free to manifest goodness in our lives. All it takes is mastering the hidden potential locked within us and taking control of our own destiny, so the universe can bring us all that we truly seek. Everything you dream of can be yours, with a little help from your crystal friends and an understanding of the law of attraction.

THE LAW OF ATTRACTION

Ancient esoteric thinkers believed "What we are is what we attract." This viewpoint implies that, whatever a person's intention or emotion, when it is thought about or felt it is projected outward and picked up as a request by the universe—only to be amplified and sent back in tangible form.

The metaphysical law of attraction, "like attracts like," states that we attract more of who or what we are into our life. Inner richness creates outer wealth and self-love generates love around us. Or, if you're miserable, bleak, and think the world is a sad place, then it will be. The more you think life does you no favors, the more that despair and hatred will be sent back to you. If you feel joy at the sight of a sunrise, believe in your talents, and have passion for achieving a goal, then the universe usually obliges. But to fully manifest what you want, you have to get your conscious mind in tune with the universe.

The current body of neuroscientific and psychological evidence also indicates that thoughts determine your destiny. In other words, if you put out positive thoughts you will attract positive experiences back into your life. If you're constantly expressing negative thoughts then you'll simply attract even more negativity back to you. If you think, believe, and act positively, you will receive positive energy in return.

THE GLUE OF UNIVERSAL ENERGY

Universal energy flows through all things, connecting everything as one. And that includes you. If you truly believe and want goodness for yourself and others, then the universe will do good for you too. Still, you can't just shrug your shoulders and think "Well, I'll just sit around imagining lots of money landing in my lap and I'll suddenly have a windfall." This might happen, but the law of probability is as relevant as the law of attraction, and this means that the coin could end up falling the "wrong" side up. So, to make sure you're putting out the right signals to the universe—both "out there" and within yourself—you must first make sure you have utter belief in yourself and the universe. But you can't believe in yourself if you aren't aware of yourself.

● Ingrained in our psyche is the belief that more money will bring us happiness. Before attempting to manifest abundance, make sure you know what kind of "wealth" you are seeking.

PRINCIPLES *of* MANIFESTATION

The principles of manifestation can be divided into seven steps, and before you start to use crystals to reinforce and amplify your intentions it's important that you are seeing things objectively. You need to be aware of what it is you truly seek, clear of all emotional and mental negativity, and open, serene, and ready for working with the power of your crystal friends.

THE SEVEN STEPS

1. SELF-AWARENESS

2. KNOWING WHAT YOU TRULY SEEK RIGHT NOW

3. AFFIRMATIONS AND INTENTION

4. BELIEF AND PASSION

5. CREATIVE ENGAGEMENT

6. TIMING AND REALISTIC GOALS

7. LETTING GO, ACCEPTANCE, AND GRATITUDE

1. SELF-AWARENESS

Before you discover how to focus on, visualize, or ask for what you seek, you need to be more aware of who you are and what you truly deserve. Most of us think we know what we desire, but we're usually brainwashed by our social, cultural, or family beliefs and opinions. We think we want this or that car, more money, or a better place to live, and that that will make us happy. Remember, the great fortune you desire may not be what you truly need or seek.

SELF-AWARENESS EXERCISE

This exercise will test you and help you to see if you really do know yourself.

WHAT YOU WILL NEED:

- Two pieces of paper
- A pen

WHAT TO DO:

1 First of all, in your own handwriting (handwriting is a powerful interface between the mind and the universe), write down a list of your weaknesses on a piece of paper. Start with key words to inspire you, such as "anger" or "fear" for the negative list. What do you get angry about? What do you fear? Start by using the following sentences as a guide. You can write as little or as much as you like for each one.

- *I HATE* ...
- *I am most UNHAPPY when* ...
- *I CAN'T BE A* ...
- *I get ANGRY when* ...
- *I DON'T WANT* ...
- *My BAD feelings arise when* ...
- *I DON'T LIKE getting* ...
- *I DON'T LIKE giving* ...

2 Now write your good qualities on a separate piece of paper. Think about key words such as "love" and "enjoyment." What do you love? What do you enjoy? Here are some sentences to complete:

- *I am most CONTENT when* ...
- *I LOVE* ...
- *I WISH for* ...
- *I ENJOY* ...
- *I am GRATEFUL for* ...
- *I NEED* ...
- *My GOOD feelings come to me when* ...
- *I have PASSION for* ...
- *I LOVE receiving* ...
- *I LOVE giving* ...
- *I am HAPPIEST when* ...

3 Have a look at your lists and think about the reactions and feelings that came to you when you wrote all this down. These are powerful symbols of YOU. Crumple up the piece of paper with the negative words on it and chuck it in the trash. Take the positive words and think them, but most of all you need to feel them—experience them as inner qualities and be aware of them and yourself. These are the "good vibrations," thoughts, and feelings which will determine your destiny.

CLEARING OUT THE DEMONS

To really be able to manifest your true desires, you have to become aware of any negativity inside you, and once aware of that, you can then dump it and replace it with positive thoughts. To do this, first accept that the world "out there" is a mirror of what goes on inside you. Who you are is what you attract and what you see in the world is who you are. Do you love the you that is you? If you don't love yourself and you're putting out "sad little old me" energy, the world will simply oblige and say back: "Yah boo sucks, sad little old you." Then you'll never be successful or happy in mind, body, or business.

First try this exercise, which will help you eliminate thought patterns that get in the way of focusing on what you seek. This exercise will help you to get rid of negative feelings, thoughts, and other emotional trash, and replace with positive life-improving energy.

WHAT YOU WILL NEED:

- A mirror
- Two pieces of paper
- A pen
- Various small crystals
- Paper bag (or similar)

WHAT TO DO:

1 Look at yourself in a mirror. What do you see? Do you like what you see? If you truly do then you can leap ahead to Step Two. If you don't like what you see in the mirror then please do the following:

- Write down a list of the things that you don't like about yourself. It might be your eyes, your feet, your weight, your frustration, your anger—or anything else.

Now, get creative with what you have written on your "don't like" list. For example, if you don't like your voice, transform it by writing something practical and positive about it. Written words magnify thoughts and help to manifest them in the tangible world. For example, write: "I'm going to start loving my unique voice," or: "I'm going to become a great singer." Or, if you hate getting up in the mornings: "I'm going to get up each morning and smile at the day, for every day is a gift."

2 Face the mirror again and look at yourself straight in the eye, saying aloud what your fears, worries, and vulnerabilities are. We all have them, so don't deceive yourself that you haven't any—that's a belief system you'd need to dump straightaway.

3 On a piece of paper, write down your list of fears, inadequacies, and any other current issues you have.

. . . .

4 Count out some small crystals (little polished ones will do)—one for each issue that you have listed. These represent the stuff that you don't want in your life and you're not going to think about any more. Because every time we think "doubt," "fear," or, "Nobody understands me," then we'll simply get doubt, fear, and misunderstanding thrown back at us.

. . . .

5 Sit down comfortably on a chair. Put the stones in a paper bag. Close your eyes and then gradually, one by one, remove them from the bag and place them on your list of negative qualities. As you remove each one affirm to yourself:

I deserve happiness just by virtue of being on this planet.

When you have finished, put your stones away safely but crumple up the paper and chuck it in the trash.

6 Now ask yourself these questions: Did you feel released from negativity when you faced your issues and dumped them? If not, you may need to do some more work in this area before you can proceed.

Do you absolutely believe that you're going to manifest your dreams and that your thoughts shape reality?

Are you someone who says "I never get," or "Why does this always happen to me?" If so, stop it now.

Start saying, "I always get" and "This is happening to me." This takes us on to positive affirmations, which can erase any self-doubt or disbelief still stuck in your mindset (see page 54).

2. KNOWING WHAT YOU TRULY SEEK RIGHT NOW

So, what is your personal "grail"? What are you truly seeking? Is it a better lifestyle, health, love, wealth, or spiritual contentment? It doesn't really matter what it is, as long as you are sure of your goal. Many people want fame or success, for example, but there are as many different kinds of success as there are individuals. Make your goal sacred but don't let it become an unobtainable distant dream. Learn to know what you want before you start to focus on it and guard it closely; like the Holy Grail of medieval legends, it should be treated with respect and hidden where nobody can find it. Only you should know what it means for you. Keep it a secret and the power of the universe will work its magic for you.

CREATIVE THINKING

Of course there is one problem. You still might not know what you truly seek. Although you are now more self-aware and have learnt how to drop negative patterns of thinking, you may have no idea how to go about finding out what your Holy Grail actually is. The following exercise will help you to access the unconscious realm of your mind, get in touch with your imagination, and allow the universe to promote a realization of what it is you are seeking.

● According to medieval legend, the Holy Grail was a sacred goblet that held Christ's blood. You must decide for yourself: What is your Holy Grail?

CONNECTING TO THE CREATIVE FORCE OF THE UNIVERSE

Make a commitment (now!) to do this simple meditational exercise every day. It doesn't have to be for long—maybe three to five minutes at a time. In the silent place you will create with this practice, where everything is connected with everything else, you will feel at one with the unlimited power of creative imagination.

Once you practice this on a regular basis, you'll notice what seems like new flashes of insight about what you are seeking. In fact, these flashes of insight are within you, but have been relegated to the unconscious part of your mind. Most of your thought processes may be taken up with negative thinking or worry, doubt, fear, or attending to what has to be done in the here and now. But after practicing meditation, you'll find the deeper insights of your mind flow up to your consciousness. Free from tangled thoughts and complexes, and with this new creative awareness, you will realize what it is you really seek, and can start to manifest it.

WHAT TO DO:

1 Relax, and find somewhere quiet and comfortable to sit. With your eyes closed, become aware of your breathing. Take slow breaths, in and out, until you feel calm and peaceful. Concentrate on your breathing.

2 Imagine each breath is like a door opening and closing. As you breathe in you are letting in beautiful thoughts and ideas. When you breathe out you are releasing dull or meaningless ones. As you breathe in, imagine the smell of roses, the smell of baked bread, or the sight of your favorite friend. As you breathe out, imagine that you're decluttering your home.

You're chucking out those unwanted nicknacks, clothes you never wear, and magazines you never read. When you breathe out, all negative thoughts, fears, or self-doubt leave too. Keep going for ten breaths, in and out. Let the good ideas continue to flow in; they'll still be there for you later.

3 Now you must empty your mind. This is challenging to begin with because thoughts will keep coming back. Use a simple technique of counting slowly to twenty in your head and focus your mind on each number. If an alien thought drifts into your head or tries to muscle in on your focused attention, you will need to start counting from the beginning again. Now, with no thoughts, imagine you are at one with the creative soul of the universe.

4 To begin with you might not find yourself in this silent place at all. But persevere. Believe you will. Soon you will find the intrusive thoughts go away simply because they can't match the source of untapped potential flowing through you. That's when you are no longer a prisoner to your thoughts and can begin to be creatively engaged in the wealth of the universe.

5 Come out of your meditative state and try to maintain an objective awareness of yourself and how your mind works throughout the day. Also, what happened to those wonderful imagined ideas you let come into your conscious mind as you breathed in? When you remember them, be creative with them. By focusing on one or all of those bright ideas and with objective self-awareness, you will soon have clarity about what it is that you truly seek.

3. AFFIRMATIONS AND INTENTION

Hopefully, by now, you are beginning to get a glimpse of your true quest, and what it is you have to manifest in your life. If not, you may need to do more self-awareness or meditational work. If you are ready to follow the pathway, then this next section provides a series of positive affirmations that will prompt you to realize that you do deserve what you desire, and that it is possible to fulfill your dreams. But what is your "intention"? It is basically your objective, your aim, your purpose. Before you can focus on that specific goal, though, you must let the universe know that your intention is for the good of the whole.

Being positive is about cutting out the negative and looking at the world with a wider perspective.

Positive affirmations, when used consistently, change our internal language pattern and eventually transform any inner negativity into a positive attitude. That means that if you really want something, and have complete faith in yourself as well as total belief that you will achieve your goal, you will get it. Remember: don't dwell on what you want, lack, or need, only on what you seek.

Here are some positive affirmations that will convince yourself and the universe that you deserve what you desire. Say them aloud and also leave them written in places that you will see every day. The more you say and think them, the more positive you will become.

POSITIVE AFFIRMATIONS

- I am filled with confidence and good intentions.
- I can transform any problem into an opportunity.
- I love myself.
- I enjoy my positive thoughts and good feelings.
- I feel grounded and in the present moment.

- I know I will succeed.
- I can handle any situation.
- I am thankful for all the good things in my life.
- I create my own lifestyle.
- I will give value to others as they will to me.
- Changing my beliefs changes my life.

Words are magical. You probably know the magic word "abracadabra" or maybe you have your own mantra—a phrase or series of words repeated over and over again to create a sense of stillness and connection to the universe. Learning to focus on your dream or goal is one of the most difficult steps in manifestation, because it is easy to be led astray by all the other rogue thoughts floating around in your head.

So, you must create a mantra of positive intention, such as "My intention is that all I seek comes to me with goodwill and the blessing of the universe." Repeat this over and over again, aloud, when you're in the car, in the bath, alone, or in a crowded place, and "think" it in your head.

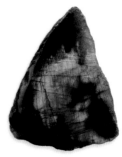

● Power stones such as labradorite enable us to focus on positive intentions.

MAGIC MANTRA RITUAL

The following exercise will help you to align yourself with your mantra and allow it to empower you with its energy.

WHAT YOU WILL NEED:

- A crystal of your choice
- A white candle

WHAT TO DO:

1 Sit in a quiet place and light the candle. It doesn't matter which crystal you use, as long as it is one that you really have an affinity for. This is a crystal for positive connection to the universe and all crystals will bring you that connection.

2 Hold your crystal between your hands and repeat your magic mantra five times. Then, place the crystal on the table in font of the candle and say aloud five times:

When I am in this still place I am connected to the affluence of the universe. I meditate each day and am no longer a prisoner to my thoughts. I am the designer of my destiny.

3 Now open your eyes and come back to your normal consciousness. Blow out the candle and relax before you answer the following questions:

- Were you aware of the creative channel flowing through you?

- After the ritual, did you feel positive about life and believe in what you seek?

If you answered "Yes" to both of these questions, you're on your way to being able to manifest your desires.

FOCUSED INTENTION

We can twist our mind to make our thoughts follow our written statements as suggested in the previous exercise (see page 55), but what will really create the flow of beneficial energy into our lives? Well, apart from the help of specific crystals, it is focused intention. So what is that exactly?

Focused intention is knowing exactly what you seek deep down inside and feeling it so powerfully that it cuts through all illusions, expectations, and doubts. It is a way of "being" rather than something thought up inside your head or outside of you. It is also about remaining emotionally detached, mentally uninvolved, and just letting the pure intention that is deep within you flow out to the universe with the aid of your chosen crystal.

Keep asking yourself what it is you truly seek. And if you can answer this question from deep down, from the heart and the soul of yourself—without ifs, buts, thoughts of "if only," hidden agendas, uncertainty,

● Concentration, belief, and focus are the keys to manifestation, but you also need to know in your heart what is right for you.

or self-sabotage—then you will manifest that intention. Once the intention is fired into the universe, via your crystal work, then you must also learn to let it go and wait for it to come to you.

So remember, to really "make it happen," intention is more than just thought. It has to be an experience within you. It's not about willing it to be or thinking it aloud. The difference is that you have to be that thought and the thought has to be you. When you know what it is you truly seek, then you can let the thought flow outward and let it go at the right moment. But you also need to start doing some practical work with crystals, too.

WHITE QUARTZ PURE INTENTION AMPLIFICATION

To help understand the difference between intention and merely hoping or willing something into existence, use a white quartz crystal to amplify the idea of pure intention and connect you to the deeper matrix of the universe.

WHAT YOU WILL NEED:

- A white quartz crystal

WHAT TO DO:

1 Sit comfortably, relax, and hold your white quartz crystal nestled between both hands. Close your eyes and concentrate on your goal or desire.

2 Ask the crystal to work with you for the good of all. Now repeat your mantra over and over again, either aloud or in your head, as you imagine that the dream you have is deep within the crystal itself.

3 As you hold the crystal, feel its power surging through you and radiating throughout your whole body. This power is flowing from the crystal in your hand but also from you. Your own power is now amplified by the white quartz crystal, so that you can do its work.

4 Before you open your eyes, ask the crystal:

Always connect me to the power of the universe, so I know what my true goal or intention is.

5 Carry the stone with you for one lunar cycle so you can really learn what that intention is.

4. BELIEF AND PASSION

Manifestation isn't just about using the law of attraction to get what you want—nor is the power of positive thinking the only thing that's needed. Positive feeling and engagement with life and the universe are necessary to bring you your heart's desire.

If you are really sure you know what you seek, and have learned how to focus your intention, the next step is to start to visualize. This isn't about imagining a mansion and suddenly receiving one. True visualization is about experiencing and being in that mental image as if it were real now. It's as if you are literally experiencing your goal at the very moment you are seeing it in your mind. You may be thinking "Can't I just say I believe in cosmic energy and make a wish?" Unfortunately, it doesn't work like that. You have to enter and become part of the mystery itself. Saying it isn't the same as believing it. Visualizing your dream or goal is another step toward manifesting it.

Like playing the guitar, the more you practice trying to "see" with your mind, the better you will get at visualizing your goal.

VISUALIZATION TECHNIQUE

Visualization techniques also promote positive creative thinking. By utilizing specific images in your mind, you are less likely to be invaded by rogue thoughts. Using these mental images is like watching a movie or gazing at a still photograph. Try sitting somewhere quiet with your eyes closed and think of something you like doing—playing tennis, eating a meal, chatting to a friend, falling in love, strumming a guitar. Now form a mental picture or simple short clip of it in your mind—whichever is easier to "see."

You can practice doing this at any time of day. The more often you practice, the more you'll prepare yourself for visualizing your dream. If you find you can't visualize like this, keep practicing and it will happen.

COLOR VISUALIZATION

Once you've got the hang of simple visualization, it's time to try the following exercise.

WHAT TO DO:

1 Sit quietly somewhere. Close your eyes and create a mental picture where you're connected to the Earth, as if your feet have roots reaching down toward the Earth's crust.

2 Now imagine that deep within the ground the color green permeates the world's interior. Realize that green is the color of manifestation.

3 Next, imagine that the color green begins to slowly work its way up through your feet, then your legs, your torso, your arms, and finally your head. Take it slowly. See the color filling you until you are completely green.

4 Now you will feel totally enriched with the goodness of the Earth. Gradually let the green color wash away, back down into the Earth.

5 If you have found that you can create the feeling of a full and enriched self by visualizing green, you will equally be able to create a feeling of utter purpose with the color red. Do the same visualization technique, simply changing the color. By changing your mental image of the world (your mindset) you can create and manifest the "color" of life that you seek.

5. CREATIVE ENGAGEMENT

Now that you can visualize what you seek, you need to learn how to make it happen. Making things happen doesn't mean waving a magic wand, but you do draw on the magic within yourself to get results. This is about engaging with the world in a creative and imaginative way. The more you trust in the process and in your own magical powers, the more likely you are to manifest those dreams. So, do a little work and see the magic happen. First, you need create the theme or "mood" of your goal or dream.

MOOD BOARD

Advertisers and designers will use a mood board—a collage of images and materials that together evoke a certain message or emotion—to create a "feel" for their range of fashion, TV set, or theater designs. Interior decorators add swashes of colors and fabrics, photos cut out of magazines, and sketches. Create your own mood board for whatever it is you seek and it will help you to focus on your goal.

You don't have to be an artist—find illustrated images that symbolize what you want, use photos of objects you dream of owning, or paint your desires on canvas if you like. The main thing is to put your passion into the mood of your collage. Then keep your mood board on your desk, in the bathroom, stuck on the fridge, or anywhere else you pass or visit frequently during the day. Every time you look at your mood board, think positively about who you are, and focus on the images as you learned to focus on your mystical mantric words. Your continued passion for and involvement with this "mood" is another key to manifestation.

⬤ Surrounding yourself with visual imagery of what you desire, or creating a mood board, will help you to believe in your quest.

IMAGINING THE OUTCOME

WHAT TO DO:

1 Create in your mind an image of what you seek. Include all the finer details, whether they're material possessions or experiences. For example, you might want to become a rich business tycoon. Picture what suit or outfit you're wearing, the kind of laptop you own, a boardroom scenario, and an amount of money in the bank, and imagine yourself running the business.

2 Devote as much time as you can each day to visualizing and concentrating on these images and thoughts. Perhaps you simply seek love and marriage. Imagine the person of your dreams, what do they look like? What color hair? What sort of eyes? What do they say to you? What do you say to them? Create your own script.

3 Practice holding the thought or vision of what you desire in your mind while you wait for the bus, or even while you tap away on the computer and another part of your brain is working. The more you exercise the visualization of what you seek, the easier it gets and the sooner you will achieve it.

● Imagining the very thing you seek is another aid to achieving it.

DAILY AFFIRMATIONS

● The following affirmations can be repeated daily, in conjunction with your visualization practice, to help you truly believe in your goals:

- *I am conscious of my thoughts, actions, and intentions.*
- *I believe and have faith in my creativity.*
- *I know that what I seek is already mine and I am grateful for that.*
- *I truly believe in what the universe will bring to me.*

To make things happen you have to feel the faith, feel the belief, and, most of all, feel the very thing you seek. This is the key to being and having it.

Allow it to come to you and it will. That's why you must without any doubt or misgiving believe in your quest and be at peace with the universe.

6. TIMING AND REALISTIC GOALS

Of course, you may think you've made all the right moves and taken all the right steps for manifesting but still feel hard done by. This may be because you need to have a realistic goal and the right timing. It is possible that the date or time you set out to achieve something by will be impractical because of energy cycles, such as the lunar cycle and other planetary influences. I'm an astrologer by trade, so I know that we can't always get what we desire exactly when we desire it—timing and realism are as much a part of the manifestation process as desire or intention.

THE BEST TIMES FOR MANIFESTATION

There are certain times that are more favorable to "fire" one's intention or practice manifestation rituals with crystals. Here are a few suggestions about when to ask for the right thing at the right time:

- Between the new crescent moon and the full moon.
- Early in the morning, at sunrise.
- On days such as the equinoxes and solstices, as long as the day doesn't occur during a waning moon.
- Your own birthday.
- When gazing at the stars at night and you see a falling star.
- A day when you simply feel at one with the universe or good to be you.
- When you get a sign from the universe. Maybe a butterfly lands on your hand, a bird sings when you least expect it, you have a moment of fascinating synchronicity—whatever feels or seems special.
- When you find a crystal that seems to say "Hey, you're magic too."
- Quiet times, when you can really relax and turn off from the material world.

We are often inspired by the deeper workings of the universe if we stop to take notice of the signs—such as a butterfly landing on us.

Finally, as well as finding the right timing, you must always ask for things you know you truly seek, not what other people think you want or what they want. Don't be led astray by impossible dreams. Be humble, gracious, grateful, and realistic.

ASK THE UNIVERSE

Here is an exercise that lets you "ask" the universe, via a crystal, whether this is a beneficial time to perform a manifestation ritual. In divination, lapis lazuli is the stone that is symbolic of the present moment. When used as part of this oracle spell, its energy draws on your deepest desire and connects you to the universe to give you the answer.

WHAT YOU WILL NEED:

- A piece of lapis lazuli
- A favorite book, such as a poetry book, Bible, or novel

WHAT TO DO:

1 Sit quietly with the lapis lazuli stone on a table in front of you, alongside your chosen closed book. Reflect for a moment about whether now is the right time to set the manifestation wheels in motion.

2 Pick up the stone. Hold it in your hands for several minutes and relax.

3 As you hold the stone, say out loud:

Is this a good time to perform my manifestation ritual?

4 Put it back on the table and now take up the book in your hands. Run your fingers back and forth along the top until you feel you are ready to open the book at a page at random. Open the book at the page, but don't look at the words yet. Place the lapis lazuli on one of the open pages, wherever it seems to guide you.

5 Now look down, remove the stone, and read the words that the lapis lazuli was covering. Treat those words as an oracle, a message which will either reveal it is good timing or not. For example, a sentence such as "It was a dark, foggy morning" sounds inert and motionless, and therefore your response would probably be: "No, this isn't a particularly good time to fire an intention." Alternatively, an active piece of writing, such as "The clouds moved fast in the sky," or "The sun rose over the mountains to the east," would imply that this is a positive and active time to get manifesting. It is up to you to intuit these kind of moments.

An oracle can be read as a sign as to whether this is an appropriate moment to act.

7. LETTING GO, ACCEPTANCE, AND GRATITUDE

Once you have released your intention into the universe, with the help of your crystal, you have to let go of it and trust in the process. If you've ever written a book or painted a work of art, you'll know how hard it is to put the pen or paintbrush down! But you have to follow the same principle here—just stop when the moment is right or you could make a mess of it.

This is often the hardest part, because most people think that if they don't keep doing the same rituals or thinking the same thoughts over and over again, nothing will happen. But repetition isn't manifestation— manifestation is knowing that it is happening from the moment you let go. How long the "happening" takes is not important. Once you can let go in this way, then you only need to hold your crystal or just smile at it to know what you seek will soon be yours.

ACCEPTANCE AND GRATITUDE

● Being creative is about self-discipline and right timing. Knowing how to finish something at the right time is as hard as starting.

In our relationship with the world we give or receive, go up and down, and move toward and away. Equally, you must balance your desire by being grateful and appreciative, not only for what you will receive but also for the desires of other people too. After all, what goes around comes around. So you must practice the art of giving out good thoughts as well as thinking them about yourself.

GENEROSITY AND GRATITUDE PRACTICE

Handwritten thank-you letters are becoming a thing of the past now that we can post our appreciation across the web in an instant. But when we write by hand, each of us creates a unique work of art on the page. This work of art is going to be your gift to the universe, and by doing this exercise you will receive as much goodness back.

WHAT YOU WILL NEED:

- A piece of paper and pen

WHAT TO DO:

1 Resolve to think only good things about anyone who comes into your mind. You may well struggle with this to begin with—"Hang on, I can't stand the boss!" But the more you think kindly of someone, the more you will be putting out positive energy that shapes your own destiny. Write down:

I think good thoughts for all.

2 Try to practice the art of giving at least once a day, by literally giving someone a flower, a smile, a compliment, a nice e-mail, praise, or genuine sympathy. Write down:

I will smile at a stranger every day.

3 Receive nature's offerings too—if it's raining be glad for it. If there's a drought know that there is meaning behind it. A drought could be ruining your livelihood but it also presents a creative opportunity to choose a change of viewpoint, to take action so that something better will come your way.

Remember to use objective perception, rather than an emotional agenda, for any problem you encounter. Write down:

I will be glad for rain, as I am for sun.

4 Name at least five things you are grateful for today. Write them down.

Now finish these phrases in your head and write them down on your piece of paper:
- *I am PLEASED when I . . .*
- *I am FASCINATED by . . .*
- *I ENJOY . . .*
- *I am GRATEFUL for . . .*
- *I DESIRE . . .*
- *WARM feelings come to me when . . .*
- *I feel JOY when . . .*
- *My PURPOSE is . . .*

● Writing down what you are thankful for is a creative engagement with the process of manifestation.

WHY CRYSTALS HELP YOU

Once you have realized how serious it is to think and feel, and to imagine yourself having the things you truly desire—and you are sure that you know what your current intention is—then you can begin to work with the crystals of your choice. There are several ways of approaching this. First, you can just use one crystal to amplify your desire (see the Crystal Sourcebook in section 3 of this book for brief guides to using each crystal on its own). As well as wearing or carrying the stone, there are other ways of reinforcing your desires. Although the most important thing is that you believe and know that you can manifest goals with your crystals, if you really want to make things happen you can get creative with a range of different crystals in the same manifestation category and use them in rituals or place them in grids. Here is a range of ways you can use crystals to help you manifest your dreams.

CRYSTALS AND SYMBOLS

When we see an ancient symbol, such as the Celtic cross, we experience an unconscious recollection that connects us to the universe and its energy.

Ancient symbols are a gateway to the unknown or invisible universe. They are a secret language and by virtue of their geometry, shape, or occult or esoteric meaning, they focus energy and amplify the power of your own manifestation magic. For example, the pentagram (see page opposite) has been a symbol of transformation and renewal, linked to Venus as the morning star and the bringer of dawn in ancient Greece.

The circle, the cross, the spiral, and the triangle are all associated with universal energy. So, placing crystals in a layout or grid in the shape of the points of the compass, or even a tarot layout such as the well-known Celtic cross, can both energize the crystal's power and add protection when left in this formation around your home.

RITUALS AND MAGIC

Before using any rituals or magic spells, it's important to be able to relax, calm your mind, and visualize what you seek. That way, the ritual or spell will be focused on your goals and the crystals used will invoke whatever energy is needed to help you on your manifestation quest.

Whether you prefer the word ritual or spell, using crystals with a series of potent movements, acts, intentions, and visualization aids will put you in harmony with the crystals and the universe. This is why combining spells and rituals with grid layouts will increase their potency tenfold.

● Thinking, feeling, and being in a positive place are the keys to the doorway to manifestation.

GRIDS AND LAYOUTS

A grid or layout is simply a geometric pattern created by placing crystals in a specific place. Grids or layouts are often used to amplify, protect, or simply to add a symbolic resonance that attunes to the universal energy flow to maximize the manifestation process. Do use the example grids in this book but, more importantly, create your own. For crystal healers, tarot readers, diviners, and astrologers alike, the geometric five-pointed star known as the pentagram is a sacred symbol that resonates with magical transformations. You may want to draw on personal favorite symbols, or a rune, hieroglyph, or sign that truly matters to you. When using the grids in this book, lay down the crystals in the order shown and when doing so, remember what you are manifesting, why you are doing so, and that the power of the universe will be brought to you as you do this. Equally, you must always respect your crystal friends and the enhancement and protection they give to you.

● The pentagram makes a perfect crystal grid, resonating to the sacred geometry of the universe.

SETTING UP a GENERATOR CRYSTAL

Before you begin working with the grids suggested in the following pages, it's useful to set up a generator crystal. This is a power source, a focal crystal that amplifies your intentions, as well as the positive effects of the other crystals used in your work. You can leave this set up on a special altar or sacred space, to work with other grids you decide to use or to continually amplify placements of crystals around the home. But where should you put it?

In the Chinese art of feng shui the southeast corner of your home is highly important for attracting wealth. But you may be seeking other forms of abundance, such as love, a fulfilling home life, spiritual happiness, or a successful business. Here is a diagram of the nine other areas of your home that correspond to different qualities you may be seeking. Set up your generator crystal and/or sacred space or altar (you can dress a table with flowers, candles, souvenirs, and so on to make it special) in the part of your home that corresponds to your current goal. This will amplify your intention to the universe.

● Each of the eight compass points corresponds to specific energies in Feng Shui. For example, if you are seeking new romance, set up your generator crystal in the southwest corner of your home to boost its power.

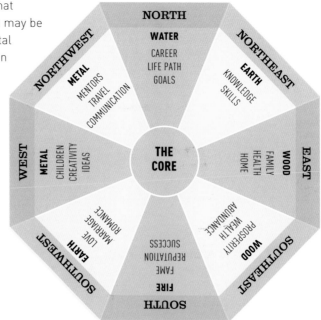

NORTH
WATER
CAREER
LIFE PATH
GOALS

NORTHWEST
METAL
MENTORS
TRAVEL
COMMUNICATION

NORTHEAST
EARTH
KNOWLEDGE
SKILLS

WEST
METAL
CHILDREN
CREATIVITY
IDEAS

THE CORE

EAST
WOOD
FAMILY
HEALTH
HOME

SOUTHWEST
EARTH
LOVE
MARRIAGE
ROMANCE

SOUTH
FIRE
FAME
REPUTATION
SUCCESS

SOUTHEAST
WOOD
PROSPERITY
WEALTH
ABUNDANCE

SETTING UP THE GENERATOR CRYSTAL

WHAT YOU WILL NEED:

- A sunny day
- A clear quartz crystal (either in the shape of a large terminated point, or a cluster of points radiating outward from the base)
- An altar, table, or sacred space in the preferred corner of your home
- Two white candles

WHAT TO DO:

1 After you have cleansed your crystal (see page 32) take it outside into the sun. If you don't have outdoor space, take the crystal to a peaceful park, quiet bit of the countryside, or beach. Stand for a few moments, eyes closed, facing toward the sun with the crystal in your hands.

2 Feel the energy of the crystal in your hands as it aligns with the solar power and repeat, in your mind or out loud, the following spell:

With this crystal all good intentions will be fired with the light of the sun and the blessing of the universe. I thank you for helping me to manifest my desire.

3 Now open your eyes and return to your altar.

4 Place the crystal between two white candles. Light the two candles and then again place your hands around the crystal, repeating the following:

With this crystal all good intentions will be fired with the power of the universe. I am at one, so all that I seek will be inspired.

5 Sit for a few moments absorbing the energy from the crystal between your hands. Then, when you are ready, let go and blow out the candles.

6 Leave the crystal in its place and occasionally perform the same generator exercise to boost your manifestation powers before using other spells, placements, or grids.

GRID TO MANIFEST ABUNDANCE

This simple grid is based on the pentagram—the five-pointed star used by medieval occultists to capture the invisible forces of the universe for magical purposes. It can be used with any abundance crystals of your choice, but to maximize prosperity, use cinnabar—the favored wealth attractor of the ancient Chinese. Meanwhile, the double-terminated clear quartz crystal will amplify the power of this grid to draw down opulent energy.

WHAT YOU WILL NEED:

- Five pieces of cinnabar (or citrine)
- A clear quartz double-terminated crystal
- An orange or yellow candle

WHAT TO DO:

1 Sit at a table. Place your crystals to the left of where you will lay them out. With focused intention (see page 56), take the candle and light it, then position it to the right of where the grid will be. As you light the candle, say out loud:

I now follow my bliss.

(Note—as you take each crystal in your hand, hold it for a few seconds and feel its power as it flows through you and the energy of your desire for abundance flows out of your hand into the crystal.)

2 Take the clear quartz crystal and place in the center of the layout and say:

I am grateful and blessed.

3 Place each of the five cinnabar crystals in the shape of a star, in the order shown on the diagram opposite, as if you were drawing a pentagram.

As you place the first crystal, say:

I accept all the joys of life and know that abundance is about being enriched within as well as without.

As you place the second, say:

I believe in myself and that I can achieve my dream of abundance.

As you place the third, say:

I will be generous with all that I have, and that means to myself too.

As you place the fourth, say:

I take pleasure in giving and receiving.

As you place the fifth say:

I ask the universe to let abundance manifest in my life.

4 Now turn the double-terminated quartz crystal in a clockwise direction so that the ends point to each cinnabar crystal in turn, until you have rotated it in a complete circle. As you do so, say:

I put my trust in the power of the universe.

5 Focus your mind on your desire for abundance for a few minutes, as you gaze at the pentangle.

6 Now blow out the candle and say:

I now let go of this intention.

7 Gradually remove all your crystals one-by-one, in the reverse order to how you first placed them. Put them somewhere safe. Keep one piece of cinnabar with you at all times, to let the process of abundance unfold.

KEY

- Cinnabar or citrine crystal
- Clear quartz

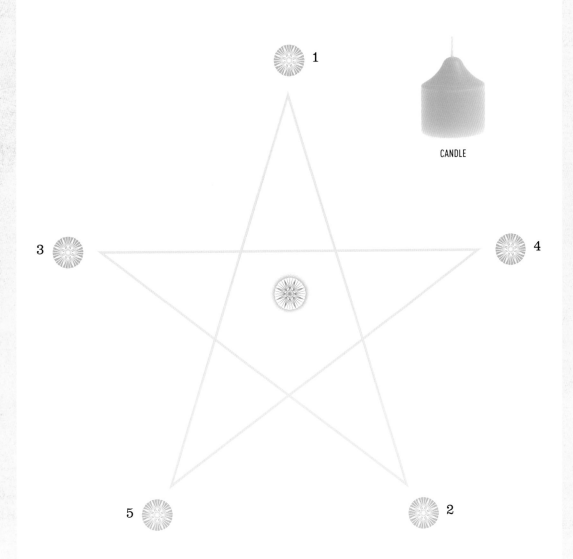

1

3

4

5

2

CANDLE

CRYSTAL SPIRAL TO ATTRACT LOVE

At times we all want to find new love, romance, rekindle a love affair, or just have a real sense of being loved and desired by someone special. This grid is designed to help you to attract the right kind of love into your life. But do you love yourself? If you're not radiating a love of yourself then you're not going to attract love. How can anyone love you if you don't? And what kind of love are you wishing to attract? If you want to be loved for being you, then self-awareness, understanding, and forgiveness are imperative qualities for attracting the right kind of attention. Without these genuine qualities, love won't come winging its way to your door.

WHAT YOU WILL NEED:

- Seven pieces of rose quartz
- Three pieces of rhodochrosite
- A pink or red candle

WHAT TO DO:

1 Before you perform this ritual, you will need to do a pre-ritual warm-up. Hold a rose quartz crystal between your hands, close your eyes, and be at peace with yourself. Feel the energy of this crystal, the rose quartz's love and acceptance, flowing through you to the deepest part of yourself, so that you feel love for yourself. Go deep within and feel your soul that loves all,

the soul that forgives and forgets, the soul that profoundly accepts the love that is given and the love you have to give too. Hold the stone until you know that you are exuding love and drawing it to you.

2 Place the seven pieces of rose quartz in the positions and order shown in the diagram. Take care to remember that this spiral draws in energy and as you place each stone say out loud what it is you wish to manifest. For example, if you seek a new lover, say:

With this crystal I bring a lover to me.

As you place the next crystal, add:

He/She will love me unconditionally, as I will him/her.

For each of the remaining five crystals, either repeat your request, or say:

I call on the universe to bring me my heart's desire.

3 Light the two candles and place one to the left of the spiral and one to the right. Now take the three pieces of rhodochrosite and place as shown in the order on the diagram.

4 As you place the last three stones, visualize what it is you desire. Sit for a minute or so and hold this vision until you are ready to let it go, then say:

I fire this intention to achieve my heart's desire, so let it be.

5 Now blow out the candles, knowing that you have sent love out to the universe and that it will come back to you as you desire.

KEY

○ Rose quartz
● Rhodochrosite

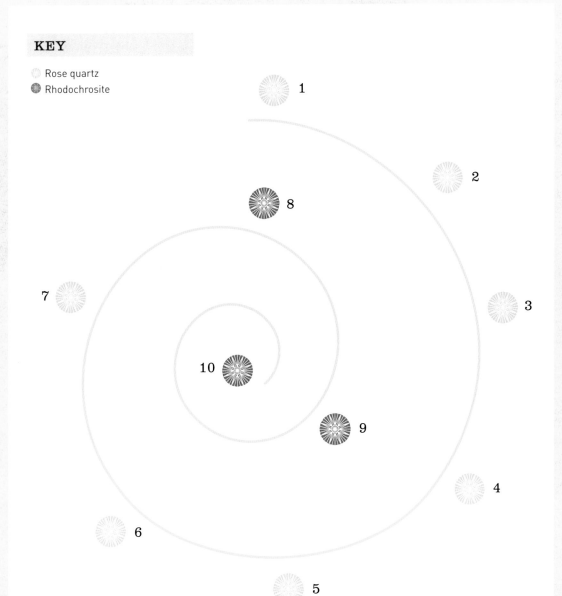

MANIFESTING HARMONY IN THE HOME

This layout or grid is based on an ancient feng shui empowerment and protection circle, signifying the points of the compass and the major cardinal directions, North, South, East, and West. By creating a protective circle in a special place in your home, this represents and attracts only positive or beneficial energy to enter your home, and banishes negative energy.

WHAT YOU WILL NEED:

- Twelve small pieces of amber
- Eight pieces of black obsidian or black tourmaline
- Four pieces of jasper
- Eight small pieces of amber
- A yellow tea-light candle or short candle

WHAT TO DO:

1 First relax, and close your eyes. Visualize in your mind how you would like your home and/or family life to be. Imagine all is peaceful, calm, and there is no stress, only comfort, warmth, and happiness. Send out these thoughts to the universe as you open your eyes and light the candle.

2 First place the four main cardinal point pieces of jasper in the order shown in a large circle around the candle (so you have room for the inner circle and connecting stones). Start with North, then East, South, then West as shown in the numbered diagram. As you place the stones at each point say:

Crystal of the North, bless this home with love and harmony. Crystal of the East, bless this home with love and harmony . . .

Continue like this around the circle:

3 Next place the outer eight pieces of black obsidian where indicated and in the order shown. These connect and direct the energy, so that the circle is complete and protected. As you place each stone, say:

Thank you universe for manifesting all that I seek for the good of the home.

4 Finally, take the remaining 12 pieces of amber for the inner circle, and the four inner connecting points, and place in the order shown. Amber 'soaks' up negative energy and any geopathic or psychic stress will be neutralised by the interconnecting power of these stones.

5 As you lay the amber pieces, say:

With these stones the universe will bring my home peace and harmony.

6 Leave the candle burning for a few minutes, and quietly sit and place your fingers on each of the stones in the outer circle to connect to the energy of the grid. Blow out the candle to fire your intention to the universe, and then leave the grid for as long as you desire to ensure harmony and peace in the home.

KEY

- Jasper
- Black obsidian
- Amber

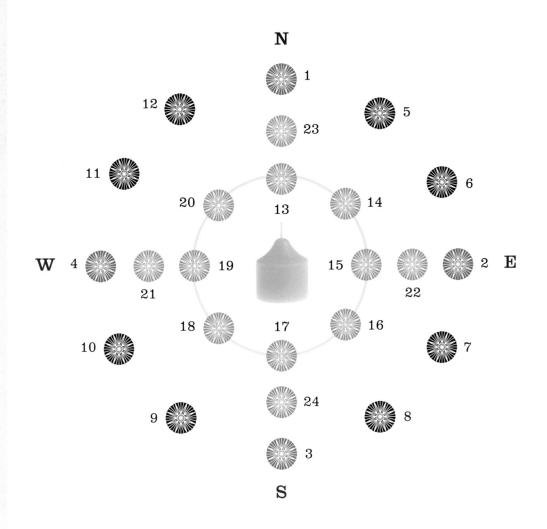

HOW TO WORK *with* THE CRYSTAL SOURCEBOOK

Now that you have begun to understand the manifestation process, there is one last thing to add into the mix: choosing the right crystals. The crystal sourcebook (pages 78–181) covers 100 crystals, divided into four categories according to their most suitable purpose. But how do you know which to choose?

CHOOSING YOUR CRYSTALS

Before you look through the crystal sourcebook, make sure that you know what you really want to manifest (see pages 52–53 and the list of guidance crystals on page 77). Once you are sure about what it is you truly seek, you can head for the relevant section of the sourcebook.

If you truly want an abundant lifestyle, then the first section, Crystals for Abundance and Good Fortune, is for you. For manifesting career goals, success, and all forms of self-empowerment, chose the Crystals for Success section. When you seek harmony, peace, holistic well-being, or a happier home and family life, chose from the Crystals for Well-Being. For positive love results, turn to the final section, Crystals for Love. All of the crystals featured can either be used alone (carried, worn, or placed in significant spots in the home) or used in tandem with other crystals in the same category. So, for example, if you are looking for wealth and prosperity, you may choose citrine, but you could also incorporate cat's eye or fire agate. You can then either create your own grids and layouts based on powerful symbols or just take a selection of crystals in a pouch wherever you go.

ATTRACTION FACTOR

For the beginner, and while you are learning about the power of manifestation that is in you, choose crystals that not only are in the "right" category for your intention but that also speak to you and stand out from the others. As you flick through the pages, you might come across one crystal that seems to be made for you, whatever category it is. You can

simply skim through each relevant section until you spot a crystal that calls out to you. Go with your instinct. Remember, what you are attracted to is also what you can attract right now.

ATTACHMENT

The 100 crystals in this book are usually available, although some may be more expensive due to their scarcity. If you can't get hold of a crystal that you feel is just right for you, don't give up on your goal. Change your focus to another more accessible crystal that will work equally well. It is all about attitude, action, and belief, and however pretty the rare crystal is or however fabulous its powers, if you can't get one now then drop the attachment and choose another. Being able to adapt and change is itself a sign to the universe that you are serious about manifesting your desire!

CRYSTALS TO GUIDE YOU

If you are still unsure about what you truly desire or seek then you can always place crystals in your home or wear them as jewelry to spark your imagination and to get you in a mindset where you can begin to focus on positive manifestation.

Sometimes we think we desire love, business success, money, or spiritual revelation, but aren't sure which. It may be that we are confused, not passionate enough about our desire, or unsure we will ever manifest it at all. This means that what we actually get in return is more doubt and confusion about our true aims. The following crystals bring clarity, truth, objectivity, or motivated ambition. They will help you to "know" the answer you seek and become sure that what you decide to manifest is right for you now.

IOLITE: *For insight*

SUGILITE: *For deep truth*

SUNSTONE: *To know your destiny*

YELLOW TOPAZ: *To be motivated*

FLUORITE: *To inspire objectivity and decisiveness*

MOSS AGATE: *To herald new beginnings and ideas*

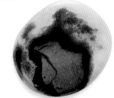

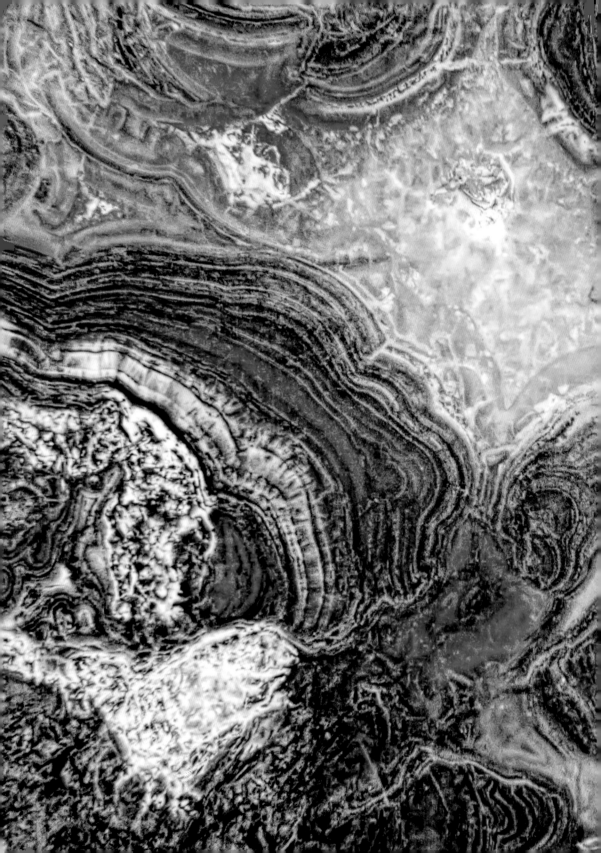

Section 3:

CRYSTAL SOURCEBOOK

· ·

Now that you have learned about the basics of crystal power and how to look after your stones, and you have practiced the seven steps to successful manifestation, it's time to find your crystal friends. The sourcebook section is divided into four categories: Abundance and Good Fortune, Success, Well-Being, and Love. Turn to the category relevant to your quest and either flip through the pages until you see a crystal that seems to call to you, or read the entries to find the one that most fits your purpose.

CRYSTALS *for* ABUNDANCE *and* GOOD FORTUNE

The crystals I identify in this section are the most empowering stones for manifesting abundance and good fortune. But what is abundance? We all say we'd like a little more of this or that and, of course, most of us would like more money. Abundance is rooted in an old Latin word meaning "fullness," "plenty," and "overflowing." So what you are hoping to manifest is to feel complete, or fortunate, or that your life is overflowing with goodness.

Whether overflowing with material wealth or spiritual wealth, what you are aiming for is to feel "full" and fortunate. Of course, this is all relative, and so when you use these crystals to feel abundant, or to attract financial wealth to you, be specific about your desires. Saying to the universe "I want more money" means you might get just a few "more" coins than you already have rather than the five thousand you intended! Remember: intention and specific details are all when it comes to manifesting good fortune.

AQUAMARINE

APPEARANCE/COLOR: *Greenish-blue*

CURRENT AVAILABILITY: *Widely available*

PHYSIOLOGICAL CORRESPONDENCE: *Hormones, immune system*

PSYCHOLOGICAL CORRESPONDENCE: *Self-confidence, tolerance, sharp mind*

ASSOCIATED CRYSTALS BY COLOR: *Emerald, dioptase*

KEYWORDS: *Dynamic results*

THE CRYSTAL

This pale blue, transparent crystal is a member of the beryl family, which includes emerald, heliodor, and golden beryl. The iron oxide inclusions in the crystal give the stone its light sea-green coloring. Found worldwide, the finest examples of aquamarine come from Brazil, China, India, Mozambique, and Zambia.

LEGENDARY USES

Roman physicians used elixirs of aquamarine as a dietery aid, to help digestion and reduce body fluid or water retention. The ancient Greeks believed the stone to be the lost treasure of sea nymphs and sirens, and so sailors carried it as a talisman for good luck, courage, and protection. Medieval seers considered it to be under the magnetic influence of the moon, and it was used as a scrying stone when the moon was waxing and believed to be at its most powerful.

ATTRIBUTES AND POWERS

Thought to promote intellectual understanding, rationalizing ability, and logic, wearing or carrying aquamarine sharpens the mind, stimulates quick-thinking, and keeps you mentally alert. It bestows not only perseverance and discipline, but also a light-hearted and tolerant view of others as well as yourself. For manifestation purposes, aquamarine enables you to break free of self-doubt, self-destructive thoughts, and brings you a dynamic sense of purpose and life direction. For manifesting abundant joy, empowering great thoughts, and for giving you the confidence to follow your dreams, the stone brings you the chances you have been waiting for.

HOW TO USE

Hold aquamarine between both your hands and meditate on your true intention. This will enhance all opportunity and bring you closer to your goal.

AVENTURINE (GREEN)

APPEARANCE/COLOR: *Green (also blue, red)*

CURRENT AVAILABILITY: *Widely available*

PHYSIOLOGICAL CORRESPONDENCE: *Thymus gland, nervous system*

PSYCHOLOGICAL CORRESPONDENCE: *Determination, reliable perception*

ASSOCIATED CRYSTALS BY COLOR: *Chrysoprase, green calcite*

KEYWORDS: *Stone of fortune, luck, prosperity, chance, and opportunity*

THE CRYSTAL

A variety of quartz (see page 99), aventurine glows with mica or other minerals that give the stone a glistening effect. Its name comes from the Italian *a ventura*, meaning "by chance." This was the name given to a type of 18th-century Italian glass produced when a worker accidentally dropped metal filings into a vat of molten glass. The same name, aventurine, was later given to the natural stone.

LEGENDARY USES

In ancient Greece, aventurine was first used in magical rituals to invoke opportunity, fortune, and luck and in medieval Europe it was known as the "gambler's stone." Up until the 19th century, aventurine was known as the "Amazon stone," as Brazilian deposits were believed to have been worked into talismans and amulets by indigenous warriors. In European folklore, green aventurine was considered to be "fairy treasure." It was believed that placing a piece in a hole in the ground alongside a broken egg would help a couple conceive a child.

ATTRIBUTES AND POWERS

Thought to be one of the luckiest of all crystals, especially in manifesting prosperity, choose aventurine when seeking abundance or wealth. Aventurine aligns external conditions to match your desires, and can bring you what you truly seek.

Psychologically, the stone is thought to help release old patterns of behavior so that you can transform your lifestyle. Carrying or wearing aventurine brings optimism and a willingness to change one's ways. It enhances creativity and motivation, and manifests perseverance and determination. Aventurine also protects against geopathic stress, heals emotional wounds, enables you to spot great opportunities, and promotes a renewed zest for life.

HOW TO USE

Place aventurine in the southeast corner of your home to bring you financial or career fortune.

CALCITE (CLEAR)

APPEARANCE/COLOR: *Clear (also available in yellow, gold, brown, green)*

CURRENT AVAILABILITY: *Common*

PHYSIOLOGICAL CORRESPONDENCE: *Bones, skin, "cure-all"*

PSYCHOLOGICAL CORRESPONDENCE: *New beginnings*

ASSOCIATED CRYSTALS BY COLOR: *Clear quartz, white beryl*

KEYWORDS: *Clarity, insight, manifests fortunate ideas*

THE CRYSTAL

Calcite is a common constituent of most sedimentary rock, particularly limestone, which was formed from the shells of marine organisms. It is often found in underground caverns, and is the major component of all stalactites and stalagmites. Found worldwide, clear calcite is crystallized calcium carbonate and is known for its double refractive quality. This can be seen if you hold a piece of crystal up to a light source—the light rays are split in two, meaning you will see two lights, not one.

LEGENDARY USES

Also known as Iceland spar, clear calcite is now believed to be the legendary "sunstone" used by the Vikings for its power to tell the position of the sun on cloudy days. The stone and the naked eye were used for navigational purposes, and the position of the sun identified to within a few degrees. A clear calcite crystal was recovered from the wreck of a 16th-century English ship, the *Alderney*, leading historians to believe this form of navigation may have continued to be used long after the 11th century, when the magnetic compass was first used by the Chinese.

ATTRIBUTES AND POWERS

Clear calcite aligns you with the universal energy flow, but also enhances balance in your life due to the crystal's double-refraction effect. For this reason, it has also been used in magic rituals to double the power of a magic spell. Similarly, calcite amplifies images, ideas, and dreams, and helps you to see double meanings hidden either in communication, or within one's own desires. As a stone of new beginnings and because of its amplifying energy, calcite manifests an abundance of ideas, and a clear perspective on where you are going in life.

HOW TO USE

Place on a sunny window ledge to double your power of manifesting abundance and good fortune.

CAT'S EYE

APPEARANCE/COLOR: *Brown, golden yellow, green*

CURRENT AVAILABILITY: *Available but expensive*

PHYSIOLOGICAL CORRESPONDENCE: *Eye disorders*

PSYCHOLOGICAL CORRESPONDENCE: *Confidence, grounding, intuitive*

ASSOCIATED CRYSTALS BY COLOR: *Tiger's eye, sunstone*

KEYWORDS: *Luck, happiness, manifests wealth*

THE CRYSTAL

The ultimate stone of luck and good fortune, the true cat's eye is a form of chrysoberyl. Cat's eye can be expensive, depending on the "line of light" that runs through the stone, giving the appearance of a cat's eye. In some stones, this effect is weak, appearing as a vague light, as opposed to a bright, concentrated band. This latter type, known as cymophane, is most commonly found in Brazil, India, Sri Lanka, and China.

LEGENDARY USES

Since ancient times, chrysoberyl has been regarded as a gemstone that keeps disaster at bay. Not only protecting its wearer against evil spirits, it has the power to enhance that person's wealth. In Russian folklore, it was advised to keep the stone in the same place where money was hidden to manifest the same amount again. In the Far East, cat's eye is now highly revered as a preserver of good fortune, guarding the owner's wealth and protecting them from poverty. In Sri Lanka, cat's eye is still considered to be a potent charm against demonic forces.

ATTRIBUTES AND POWERS

When acquiring a true cat's eye make sure that the "eye" has a fine line running right through it, and the crystal should be of a distinctive color and as transparent as possible. The most popular ones are a beautiful honey yellow or with fine green tones. Associated with wealth, cat's eyes are said to bring fortune and riches, and also enable the wearer to think clearly and with foresight. Thanks to the magical powers of the cat's eye, negative thoughts are said to be transformed into positive energy. A precious cat's eye will help you manifest financial and material abundance.

HOW TO USE

Wear or carry on the right side of your body to boost your desire for abundance. You can also place it in the center of a ritual grid to bring positive energy to your intentions.

CINNABAR

APPEARANCE/COLOR: *Crimson red, brown, russet*

CURRENT AVAILABILITY: *Available but expensive*

PHYSIOLOGICAL CORRESPONDENCE: *Blood purification*

PSYCHOLOGICAL CORRESPONDENCE: *Empowerment, assertiveness*

ASSOCIATED CRYSTALS BY COLOR: *Ruby, fire agate*

KEYWORDS: *Prosperity, abundance, favorable investment*

THE CRYSTAL

Cinnabar has a symmetrical structure similar to quartz and is found in a granular or earthy form. Because of its toxic mercury content, buy only tumbled or polished stones. It is found worldwide and is usually crimson or brick-red in color but the finest examples of red cinnabar are sourced from China, Spain, and the USA.

LEGENDARY USES

Often known as the "merchant's stone," an ancient Chinese belief holds that placing it among your financial papers will bring increased wealth to your business. The ancient Mayan peoples used cinnabar in their jewelry and powdered it down to be burnt at funeral rites. This would create transformative energy to aid the dead to pass to the afterlife. Cinnabar was known to have been mined in the ancient Roman settlement of Almadén, Spain, where miners' lives were miserably short, owing to the toxicity of the stone.

ATTRIBUTES AND POWERS

Also known as a stone of transformation, cinnabar helps to manifest changes in the world around you. Enhancing your self-esteem, it empowers you and attracts successful people to you. Once a popular stone used in alchemy and magic spells, cinnabar aligns your energy with that of the universe, unblocks negativity, and allows free-flowing abundance into your life. The stone promotes inspired thinking, communication, and enhances all forms of trade and negotiation. The psychological "magic" of cinnabar is that it opens doors of opportunity, while closing others, consigning them to the past. It is a powerful manifestation crystal for future prosperity.

HOW TO USE

Cinnabar should be placed in a box with some money to manifest abundance and wealth. Either lock the box or hide it away from family members, due to its mercury content. Because of its toxicity, it is no longer used either as a pigment or jewelry.

CITRINE

APPEARANCE/COLOR: *Light yellow to yellowish brown*

CURRENT AVAILABILITY: *Natural citrine is rare; heat-treated quartz is more widely available*

PHYSIOLOGICAL CORRESPONDENCE: *Digestive system*

PSYCHOLOGICAL CORRESPONDENCE: *Self-expression, enthusiasm, creativity*

ASSOCIATED CRYSTALS BY COLOR: *Yellow sapphire, yellow jasper*

KEYWORDS: *Abundance, self-belief, true prosperity, joy, and passion attractor*

THE CRYSTAL

Found worldwide, this transparent yellow variety of quartz is often a heat-treated form of amethyst. Rather than diluting the crystal's power, this process tends to enhance it. However, the lighter yellow and purer the color, the more likely it is to be natural citrine. The major source is Brazil, but citrine is also found in Argentina, France, Spain, and Scotland.

LEGENDARY USES

In ancient Greece, citrine was often mistaken for topaz, and was used by many ancient civilizations, such as the Babylonians, in beautiful jewelry and intaglio work. Fashioned into exquisite jewelry in the 19th century, it then became hugely popular during the Art Deco period of the 20th century. Prized pieces of citrine were worn by the celebrities of the day including Greta Garbo and Joan Crawford.

ATTRIBUTES AND POWERS

Sparkling yellow citrine is the stone of abundance and manifestation, attracting wealth and prosperity, success, and all things fabulous to you. It also encourages generosity and the ability to share in your good fortune. Often called the "success stone," it is said to promote good luck in all you do. Citrine never needs cleansing as it dispels all negative energy, and can clear unwanted energies such as geopathic stress and psychic pollution from the environment. If you can get hold of real "natural citrine," this is the ultimate manifestation stone, empowering your imagination, and removing all negativity. Embodying the power of the sun, citrine is a dynamic, joyful, optimistic stone, which if worn or carried will bring you positive results.

HOW TO USE

Wear or carry in your purse or pocket to enhance your vibrant spirit and attract good fortune in whatever you do.

COPPER

APPEARANCE/COLOR: *Copper brown*

CURRENT AVAILABILITY: *Widely available*

PHYSIOLOGICAL CORRESPONDENCE: *Circulation*

PSYCHOLOGICAL CORRESPONDENCE: *Optimism, diplomacy*

ASSOCIATED CRYSTALS BY COLOR: *Smoky quartz, red sardonyx*

KEYWORDS: *Good luck, abundant chances*

THE CRYSTAL

Although not technically a crystal, copper is a metal mineral with similar powers to all other crystals and minerals, and has been used for thousands of years for mind, body, and spirit healing. It is an important mineral for manifesting abundance.

LEGENDARY USES

Copper was first mined in Egypt and Sumeria as far back as 3900 BCE. The Egyptians were among the first civilizations to use copper, tin, and bronze for utensils and by 2500 BCE it was often the major component of adornment, jewelry, and other decorative ware. It has worldwide appeal and can be found everywhere from South and Central America, the southern part of North America, to the Far East, and Europe. Known for its power to restore balance to the physical body, it was also thought to ward off evil, particularly in medieval Christian lore.

ATTRIBUTES AND POWERS

Copper is a conductor of heat and electricity, and similarly it is also considered a conductor of spiritual energy, enabling it to flow between people, their auras, and the universe. Wearing copper enables you to combat laziness and lethargy, and to accept your true nature. Stimulating optimism, initiative, independence, and diplomacy, it is more importantly thought to be the bringer of good luck. Notably, copper is said to bring positive energy in the recovery of property or possessions when lost or fallen into the wrong hands. Wearing or carrying copper also attracts money, abundance, and invokes a powerful sense of wealth.

HOW TO USE

Scatter some old copper coins on the floor discreetly under a rug or cupboard, to attract money to you. Or wear a copper bracelet and by doing so you will align yourself to the abundance of the universe.

DIAMOND

APPEARANCE/COLOR: *Clear white, yellow, brown*

CURRENT AVAILABILITY: *Available but very expensive*

PHYSIOLOGICAL CORRESPONDENCE: *Brain, metabolism, eyes*

PSYCHOLOGICAL CORRESPONDENCE: *Fortitude, fearlessness*

ASSOCIATED CRYSTALS BY COLOR: *Clear quartz crystal, clear sapphire, zircon*

KEYWORDS: *Empowerment, abundant beginnings*

THE CRYSTAL

The hardest natural substance known, the diamond is composed of pure carbon. This brilliant stone is crystallized deep in the Earth's mantle under intense heat and pressure and most are found in India, Australia, and Africa. Derived from the Greek *adamas*, meaning "unbreakable," and *diaphanus*, meaning "transparent," the diamond is exactly that.

LEGENDARY USES

Since antiquity, the diamond has been known as the "stone of invincibility." Whoever wore it was thought to be blessed with superior strength, fortitude, and courage. The first-century CE Roman writer Pliny considered the diamond would not only protect its wearers, but make them invincible—a belief echoed by writers in later centuries. If worn on the left side, a lord, king, or courtier would be victorious whether in court or in war, as long as his cause was just. Wearing a diamond also protected him from riots, wild beasts, and storms, and drove away ghosts, demons, and nightmares.

ATTRIBUTES AND POWERS

Associated with fearlessness, the diamond is the ultimate symbol of wealth and manifesting abundance in one's life. It is a powerful amplifier of your desires, goals, and intentions, and can also be used to magnify the vibrations of other healing crystals. Wearing a diamond amplifies your charisma, radiating goodness all around you, and attracting it back tenfold. Positive reactions from others mean you have more opportunities to attract prosperity. However, diamonds can increase negative energies as well as positive, so make sure that your desire for abundance is for the good of everyone around you. As a symbol of wealth, diamonds can truly be said to be a girl's best friend.

HOW TO USE

Wear a single diamond as a ring or as pendant when you seek to attract useful mentors, contacts, or opportunities to you.

FIRE AGATE

APPEARANCE/COLOR: *Deep red to brown with iridescent flashes*

CURRENT AVAILABILITY: *Widely available*

PHYSIOLOGICAL CORRESPONDENCE: *Digestive system*

PSYCHOLOGICAL CORRESPONDENCE: *Creativity, sexual self-expression*

ASSOCIATED CRYSTALS BY COLOR: *Cinnabar, ruby, copper*

KEYWORDS: *Zest for living, passionate desires, enhanced charisma, fame, and fortune*

THE CRYSTAL

Fire agate is a variety of chalcedony, a mineral of the quartz family. It has a translucent, reddish-brown base, with flame-like flashes of orange, red, green, and gold, which add to its association with fire. Its iridescent colors are caused by light refraction on thin layers of iron oxide within the stone.

LEGENDARY USES

In ancient Greece, fire agate amulets were worn as a protection against all danger, and were used in magic spells to change the weather or banish storms and droughts. Later, the Romans used the stone as both a talisman and for its medicinal qualities—in powdered form it was said to be an antidote for serpent's venom. It was also used by medieval alchemists, as this particular form of agate was thought to contain the essence of pure fire. Throughout antiquity and well into the medieval period, fire agate was carried by sailors as protection against treacherous ocean currents or monstrous waves, particularly in medieval Christian lore.

ATTRIBUTES AND POWERS

Corresponding to the symbolic element of fire, the stone not only fires up your interest in life, it promotes passion for everything you desire. It enables you to take decisive action, be sure of your quest, and focus your intention. With its power to fuel you both with emotional power as well as mental courage, fire agate connects you to your deepest longings, and gives you the impulse to take the right risks to fulfill your dreams. Not only is the stone beneficial in self-acceptance, but promotes self-confidence, and more importantly, communicating successfully what you truly believe. Overcoming negativity, resentment, or bitterness, fire agate dissolves anger, promotes love, and gives you the chance to bring abundance into your life.

HOW TO USE

To attract fame, or an abundant career or lifestyle, place in a north corner or north-facing window of your home.

GOLDSTONE

APPEARANCE/COLOR: *Glittering golden brown, blue, or green*

CURRENT AVAILABILITY: *Widely available*

PHYSIOLOGICAL CORRESPONDENCE: *Circulatory system, bones*

PSYCHOLOGICAL CORRESPONDENCE: *Stability, drive, ambition*

ASSOCIATED CRYSTALS BY COLOR: *Citrine, fire opal*

KEYWORDS: *Prosperity, luck*

THE CRYSTAL

Thought to be invented by a 17th-century Venetian glassmaker, goldstone, sometimes known as the "money stone," is not a natural crystal at all, but made by adding copper mineral to molten glass. The flecks of copper create the stone's dramatic sparkling effect.

LEGENDARY USES

Some say that the man-made stone was first created by medieval alchemists in their quest to turn base metal into gold. Others believe that it was originally made by Italian monks to a secret recipe, and was known as "monk's gold." Whatever its origins, in the 19th century goldstone was used for "nanny brooches." These were awarded by wealthy Victorian families to their nannies who could then show off their status as they strolled the parks of London with babies in brand-new perambulators. The goldstone was usually a lovely medium-size piece set on a bar of brass, which unscrewed to house a tiny sewing kit.

ATTRIBUTES AND POWERS

Known as a stone of ambition and strength or purpose, goldstone also calms and stabilizes erratic moods and emotions. Helping you to attain your goals, it also banishes unwanted energies, including geopathic stress and psychic negativity around the home or workplace. Its greatest power lies in its ability to manifest abundance and good fortune. Symbolic of the fierce heat of the creation of the universe, as well as the alchemical magic of turning lead into gold, similarly the stone promotes the transformation of a basic idea into a golden opportunity. When used in rituals or carried with you, goldstone enables you to realize your ideas, whether for prosperity, new opportunities, or good luck.

HOW TO USE

Carry with you in your pocket: when you have a good feeling about wishing something, hold the stone between your hands, make that wish, and it will come true.

HELIODOR

APPEARANCE/COLOR: *Gold, yellow*

CURRENT AVAILABILITY: *Available but can be expensive*

PHYSIOLOGICAL CORRESPONDENCE: *Pulmonary and circulatory systems*

PSYCHOLOGICAL CORRESPONDENCE: *Courage, strength, self-belief*

ASSOCIATED CRYSTALS BY COLOR: *Citrine, yellow sapphire*

KEYWORDS: *Manifests abundant ideas; what matters to you*

THE CRYSTAL

Beryls are in their rawest state colorless, but their silicate structure is easily tainted by chemicals and minerals, and it is these which give rise to various colors—including the prized members of the beryl family, emerald and aquamarine (see pages 17 and 81). Heliodor or golden beryl comes in all shapes and sizes, although it is usually prismatic or pyramidal, and for the purposes of manifestation for success, its golden, yellow hue is the perfect friend.

LEGENDARY USES

The stone's name, heliodor, derives from the Greek word meaning "gift of the sun." The ancient Greeks believed the stone contained the power of the original sun god, Helios, as he drove the solar chariot across the sky every day. The Roman author Pliny recorded how powdered beryl was used to cure eye injuries, protect travelers from danger, and maintain youthfulness. As a magical stone in medieval Europe, beryl was used to manifest the image of angels or spirits who would answer oracular questions.

ATTRIBUTES AND POWERS

Golden beryl raises your self-esteem and empowers you with positive energy. This is the stone which will reveal to you exactly what you need to do and it is perfect for manifesting specific goals. Apart from its power to bring courage and confidence, it promotes a positive view of the world and your place in it. Beryl also stops you from "over-thinking" and subdues anxiety. As a healing stone it is a sedative, but it can literally awaken love in any dull relationship. Golden beryl stimulates initiative and the desire to succeed. It also increases sincerity and truth of your goals.

HOW TO USE

Place on a window ledge where it can draw on solar energy by day, to attract abundance. If you are in doubt about a career goal, ask the stone and trust what first pops into your mind.

JADE (LIGHT GREEN)

APPEARANCE/COLOR: *Light green*

CURRENT AVAILABILITY: *Widely available*

PHYSIOLOGICAL CORRESPONDENCE: *Kidneys, filtration*

PSYCHOLOGICAL CORRESPONDENCE: *Creativity, self-confidence, realism*

ASSOCIATED CRYSTALS BY COLOR: *Green aventurine, aquamarine*

KEYWORDS: *Empowerment, good luck, fortune, wisdom*

THE CRYSTAL

There are two sorts of jade available. The most common, nephrite, is either creamy white or mid- to deep olive green with a smooth surface polish. It is made up of calcium and magnesium and is commonly found in China. The harder, more lustrous, and rarer jadeite comes in white, gray, red (see page 124) and varying shades of green and is found in Myanmar. The lightest greens and yellow jadeite, known as "imperial jade," are the most expensive. Jadeite is made up of aluminum and sodium.

LEGENDARY USES

In the ancient Far East, jade was—as it still is—revered as a precious, lucky stone. It was though to be associated with yang energy and the ten solar gods of Chinese mythology. One Chinese alchemist believed that jade-studded gold talismans, placed in the nine openings of a deceased's body, would purify and prevent it from decomposing. Inspiring mental agility and promoting quick decision-making, ancient Far Eastern traders would hold jade in the palm of the right hand while making business transactions.

ATTRIBUTES AND POWERS

A sacred stone, jade has long been highly valued in China, honored for its beauty, powers of healing, and associations with prosperity, and worn for protection. Carved or otherwise worked into gems, ritual items, statues, and jewelry, jade also bestows the owner or wearer with confidence, self-reliance, and self-sufficiency. Emotionally, jade is used to banish negative thoughts, ease irritability, and calm high tempers. When worn or carried, it also balances mind and body, and stimulates new ideas. For manifestation purposes it is the perfect power stone to attract abundance and prosperity, bringing you a charismatic aura, a nose for opportunity, and bestowing you with lucky chances.

HOW TO USE

Wear every day or place green jade on your desk and hold or touch it regularly. It radiates your good spirit and in return attracts goodness back.

JASPER (RED)

APPEARANCE/COLOR: *Reddish brown*

CURRENT AVAILABILITY: *Common*

PHYSIOLOGICAL CORRESPONDENCE: *Liver, sexual function, reproductive organs*

PSYCHOLOGICAL CORRESPONDENCE: *Insight, sense of proportion*

ASSOCIATED CRYSTALS BY COLOR: *Ruby, red carnelian*

KEYWORDS: *Assertion, balance, confidence*

THE CRYSTAL

Jasper is a variety of quartz formed with grain-like crystals rather than the fibrous layering of other crystals such as agate. Found the world over, its best-known colors of vibrant red to terracotta are caused by its high iron content, and it may contain other minerals which can form intricate patterns.

LEGENDARY USES

To ancient civilizations, red jasper was associated with blood, and to the Egyptians, specifically with the blood of the goddess Isis. Made into protective amulets, the stone was placed on the neck of the deceased to ward off evil in the afterlife. Native American indigenous people used red jasper to promote good health and aid with birth. Shamans often wore the stone or used it as a dowsing pendulum when searching for underground water or in ritual grids when calling in rain. In ancient Greece, the third-century BCE poet Posidippus called the stone "misty jasper, the ethereal stone," retelling the ancient Mesopotamian creation myth that one of the spheres of the heavens was formed from jasper.

ATTRIBUTES AND POWERS

Jasper is used to counter geopathic stress as well as for dowsing. But it comes into its own for manifesting abundance. The stone connects dreams, ideals, and ideas with down-to-earth realism, and allows you to transform your life with self-belief, assertive power and to stay in harmony with others. Holding or carrying jasper will remind you that to create abundance in your life, you must freely give out opulent love to those around you and the universe too. The stone bestows you with courage and determination to transform initial ideas into practical action.

HOW TO USE

Place in the northeast corner of your home to attract wisdom, skill, and knowledgeable contacts to boost your transformative powers.

KAMBABA JASPER

APPEARANCE/COLOR: *Green and mottled brown*

CURRENT AVAILABILITY: *Available but expensive*

PHYSIOLOGICAL CORRESPONDENCE: *Nervous system*

PSYCHOLOGICAL CORRESPONDENCE: *Creativity, growth, strength*

ASSOCIATED CRYSTALS BY COLOR: *Green aventurine, malachite*

KEYWORDS: *Attracting a flourishing career, abundant opportunity*

THE CRYSTAL

Kambaba jasper is not strictly a jasper at all, but is made up of a network of quartz, feldspar, amphibole, and ancient fossil colonies created by three billion-year-old microorganisms known as stromatolites. Despite its ancient heritage, the stone has become available only recently and is sourced from Madagascar and southern Africa.

LEGENDARY USES

As a recent discovery, there are no legends about this stone, but its common name, crocodile jasper, in reference to its resemblance to crocodile skin, suggests it can also be likened to the sudden movements of a crocodile, which is able to seize its prey with a lightning snap of its jaws. In other words, this is an opportunist's stone. As kambaba jasper is a rare find, keep this stone safely in your home or pocket, it can invite and attract favorable chances and circumstances to you.

ATTRIBUTES AND POWERS

This stone may be used to increase money flow and prosperity in your life. Kept in the workplace, it improves an already established career or business interest, and wards off any unnecessary or unwanted changes. It is a potent stone for making quick decisions, changing plans, and kick-starting any new project or business venture. Kambaba jasper is perfect for keeping a venture on course, a project on schedule, and life on track. It is a talisman of physical growth and strength, and also bestows the wearer safety in travel.

HOW TO USE

Place in the southeast corner of your desk or workplace and watch abundant opportunities arise in your life.

LABRADORITE

APPEARANCE/COLOR: *Gray-green, black, blue-gray*

CURRENT AVAILABILITY: *Widely available*

PHYSIOLOGICAL CORRESPONDENCE: *Eyes, brain, metabolism*

PSYCHOLOGICAL CORRESPONDENCE: *Self-assurance, self-belief, strength of mind*

ASSOCIATED CRYSTALS BY COLOR: *Idocrase, lapis lazuli*

KEYWORDS: *Seizing opportunity, synchronicity, magical change*

THE CRYSTAL

Discovered in Canada by Moravian missionaries in the 18th century and named after the region known as Labrador, the stone is a type of feldspar. Composed in aggregate layers, the stone refracts light as unusual iridescent flashes of blue, gold, green, and copper.

LEGENDARY USES

The magical northern lights (aurora borealis) were once thought by the Inuit peoples of Canada and Alaska to consist of frozen fire. As the mysterious phenomenon appeared in the skies, it was believed that fragments of the iced fire fell to Earth and appeared as labradorite. Often referred to as the "stone of magic," for centuries it has been used as by shamans, diviners, healers, and magicians and all who seek knowledge and guidance from the universe. Labradorite was considered to be a talismanic gem of winter, and in Chinese culture it is a highly regarded and auspicious stone due to its extraordinary iridescence, which is considered to bring good fortune to the person wearing it.

ATTRIBUTES AND POWERS

Labradorite is the stone of self-discovery. It awakens you not only to your inner spiritual power, but helps you to use your intuition and develop your psychic abilities. Holding the crystal between your hands helps you focus, amplifies your desires, and simultaneously protects you from outside negativity, such as psychic attack from others who may envy your quest. Once this stone shimmers with extraordinary colors, it reminds you that you too can create an abundance of "colorful" opportunities in your life. It can also bring you extraordinary abundance of spiritual fulfillment and the power to be in the right place at the right time, so the wheel of fortune will turn favorably for you.

HOW TO USE

Form a circle with five pieces of labaradorite surrounding a central piece, light a candle, close your eyes, and ask for "the right time and place to materialize my dreams."

MALACHITE

APPEARANCE/COLOR: *Dark green*

CURRENT AVAILABILITY: *Widely available*

PHYSIOLOGICAL CORRESPONDENCE: *Joints, muscles, immune system*

PSYCHOLOGICAL CORRESPONDENCE: *Emotional healing*

ASSOCIATED CRYSTALS BY COLOR: *Green tourmaline, green aventurine*

KEYWORDS: *Transformation, protection, inner insight*

THE CRYSTAL

The name malachite may come from the Greek words *malache*, meaning "like mallow leaves," or *malakos*, meaning "soft." Whatever the case, malachite is a copper carbonate mineral like azurite, and was used as a pigment in green paints from antiquity until about 1800. Historically, it has been considered a magical stone for healing and protection work.

LEGENDARY USES

To empower Egyptian pharaohs with divine wisdom, malachite was used to line the outside of their ornate headdresses. Also worn as amulets engraved with the symbol or image of the sun, the stone became a powerful talisman and protected the wearer from enchantment, evil spirits, and venomous creatures. Throughout Europe from Roman times, the crystal became a protective amulet for children and was used to counter the "evil eye." A piece of malachite attached to an infant's cradle warded off evil spirits and the child could sleep peacefully.

ATTRIBUTES AND POWERS

Being a stone of transformation, malachite enhances spiritual growth, but is also a protection stone, absorbing negative energies and pollutants from both the atmosphere and the body. It guards against radiation of all kinds, clears electromagnetic pollution, and eliminates negative earth energies. For manifestation purposes, malachite enables you to let go of the past and revise your expectations of what it is you truly seek. Known for its ability to attract wealth, it brings richness of mind, body, spirit, and soul, and restores your own magical power to attract abundance in your life.

HOW TO USE

Place three polished stones in a pyramid shape (the point to the top), write the word "abundance" on a scrap of paper, place in the center, and leave on a southeast-facing window ledge to gather the power of fortune to you.

MOSS AGATE

APPEARANCE/COLOR: *Green-blue, sometimes with red or cream flecks*

CURRENT AVAILABILITY: *Widely available*

PHYSIOLOGICAL CORRESPONDENCE: *Anti-inflammatory*

PSYCHOLOGICAL CORRESPONDENCE: *Self-expression, optimism, insight*

ASSOCIATED CRYSTALS BY COLOR: *Green selenite, green quartz*

KEYWORDS: *Fertile ideas, abundant rewards, flourishing life*

THE CRYSTAL

Said to resemble moss growing on trees, moss agate is not an agate, but a variety of chalcedony, belonging to the quartz family. It is clear to milky white, with a dendritic (branching) structure of manganese or iron that give rise to the lichen or mosslike patterns. Spots of red may occur in some specimens, and occasionally the crystal is dark green with bluish inclusions.

LEGENDARY USES

Moss agate was used by ancient European witches and seers to insure flourishing crops. Considered to be a miraculous healing stone, it was used by indigenous American shamans to cure almost any disease, and as a talisman to make warriors strong and victorious. With its reputation to heal all wounds and, as an elixir, to be an antidote to poisons, it was also believed to protect against venomous reptiles. According to medieval magicians, wearing the stone would increase longevity, and aid the wearer in warding off anger and dark thoughts.

ATTRIBUTES AND POWERS

Known for its benefits to help with productive harvests and the trade of agricultural produce, moss agate promotes abundance in all things, whether in the garden or home life. If you grow your own tomatoes, literally placing the stone in the pot can encourage the plant to produce more fruit than a normal fertilizer! Moss agate helps to ground and stabilize moods and fears, but most importantly, it is a stone of wealth and prosperity. In the workplace, it can promote new business and aid any form of enterprise expansion. Beneficial for small businesses, it is also a lucky crystal for financial institutions.

HOW TO USE

Placing moss agate amongst your financial papers or bank statements promotes savings and solvency.

PERIDOT

APPEARANCE/COLOR: *Green, yellow-green, olive*

CURRENT AVAILABILITY: *Common*

PHYSIOLOGICAL CORRESPONDENCE: *Respiratory tract, lungs, metabolism*

PSYCHOLOGICAL CORRESPONDENCE: *Stress-reduction, forgiveness*

ASSOCIATED CRYSTALS BY COLOR: *Green aventurine, Emerald*

KEYWORDS: *Awakens you to what you truly desire*

THE CRYSTAL

Peridot is formed in molten rock of the upper mantle beneath the Earth's crust, and brought to the surface by the tremendous forces of earthquakes and volcanoes. Depending on the amount of iron found in the stone, various shades of green determine its other names: olive green is known as olivine, yellow-green is chrysolite, and lightest green, peridot.

LEGENDARY USES

Peridot has been prized since the earliest civilizations for its protective powers to drive away the forces of darkness. Usually worn as an amulet set in gold, it was used as a charm against sorcery, black magic, evil spirits, and demonic possession. It was said to cure cowardice, calm anger, and brighten the wit. The Renaissance magician Cornelius Agrippa declared that a peridot held to the sun would shine forth "a golden star" to soothe the respiratory system and cure asthma. It became a popular powder used in 16th-century apothecary stores as an antidote to madness, as well as a cure for respiratory problems, lack of sleep, and nightmares.

ATTRIBUTES AND POWERS

Peridot not only sharpens the mind, but gives you the confidence to rely on yourself rather than on outside influences. Wearing the stone instills a sense of purpose and clarity, and empowers you with the intention to create what you truly seek in life. Both mentally stimulating and physically regenerating, peridot opens you to new levels of awareness and growth, so you can realize your destiny or spiritual purpose. It not only gives you a sense of self-worth, it also enables you to manifest abundance in all areas of your life, whether its wealth, career affluence, or simply bountiful happiness.

HOW TO USE

Place five pieces of peridot in a circle around a piece of white quartz crystal and, with daily blessings, see your life change for the better.

QUARTZ (CLEAR)

APPEARANCE/COLOR: *Clear*

CURRENT AVAILABILITY: *Readily available*

PHYSIOLOGICAL CORRESPONDENCE: *Immune system, all-healer*

PSYCHOLOGICAL CORRESPONDENCE: *Concentration, focus*

ASSOCIATED CRYSTALS BY COLOR: *Diamond, selenite*

KEYWORDS: *Being at one with the universe, amplifying and manifesting intentions*

THE CRYSTAL

Clear quartz, or pure silicon dioxide, is the champion of the silicates and its exceptional vibrationary power means that larger examples can be quite expensive. The prismatic hexagonal crystals have smooth sides and faceted terminations at one or both ends. They may be as transparent as glass, milky, or striated, and often found in clusters and ranging in all sizes.

LEGENDARY USES

In ancient Rome, quartz was believed to be solidified ice, and wealthy ladies carried crystal balls to cool their hands in the hot summer weather. In Central and South American cultures, quartz crystals were carved in the shapes of human skulls. Venerated as powerful religious objects, they were placed in the home of deceased ancestors. The first-century Christian mystic, Apollonius of Tyana, allegedly owned a crystal ball which made him invisible at will, and was believed to have demonstrated his power in front of Caesar.

ATTRIBUTES AND POWERS

Clear quartz is excellent for amplifying the energies of other stones or to enhance groups of stones, and is an ideal central stone in grids. It also restores balance to the body, strengthens metabolism, and is a powerful anti-inflammatory. Working on every level of being, quartz attunes to your desires and emotional needs, and can be used for all forms of spiritual healing. Connecting you to the highest vibrations of the universe, it is a powerful manifestation stone, but it's very important you know exactly what you are seeking, and focus your intention in the most positive way. With this crystal, what you ask from the universe, you usually get.

HOW TO USE

When held, carried, or worn, clear quartz brings strength and self-belief. Also, place in the center of a grid to amplify other stones, such as citrine, for manifesting fortune.

SPINEL (RED BURMESE)

APPEARANCE/COLOR: *Red and shades of red-orange*

CURRENT AVAILABILITY: *Available but expensive*

PHYSIOLOGICAL CORRESPONDENCE: *Joints, bones, muscles,*

PSYCHOLOGICAL CORRESPONDENCE: *Charisma, success*

ASSOCIATED CRYSTALS BY COLOR: *Red carnelian, garnet*

KEYWORDS: *Creating positive outcomes, attracting achievement*

THE CRYSTAL

Composed of magnesium aluminate, red Burmese spinel gives off a strong reddish-orange fluorescence when exposed to UV light and the stone literally glows in daylight. This flaming stone brings charisma to the wearer, and you will literally feel as if you are glowing from some great fire within.

LEGENDARY USES

Only recognized since around 1850, spinels were once thought to be rubies. In fact, many of the world's historically famous rubies are actually ruby-red spinel, including the magnificent red spinel that adorned Henry V's battle helmet which, according to legend, deflected a blow that would likely have killed him. Another such stone, the Samarian Spinel, weighing 500 carats and measuring over 2 inches (5 cm) wide, is believed to have adorned the neck of the Biblical golden calf. It is now part of the Iranian crown jewels.

ATTRIBUTES AND POWERS

Red, pink, or orange spinel cuts through our illusions and sends flashes of intuitive understanding about what we truly need or desire in life. It promotes thoughts and creative ideas, as well as attracting whatever help is needed to unravel problems or create a positive outcome. Wearing spinel enhances your personal energy, emotional strength, and self-belief, and protects you from the negative influences of others. Spinel may also be worn to attract money, wealth, and abundance. To deal with difficult people, promote your career, or show that you won't be a walk-over in any business deal or dilemma, wear red spinel and energize your power.

HOW TO USE

Best worn and carried with you whenever you want to radiate charisma to attract your greatest desire.

SUNSTONE

APPEARANCE/COLOR: *Red, brown, orange*

CURRENT AVAILABILITY: *Common, but pure red rare*

PHYSIOLOGICAL CORRESPONDENCE: *Metabolism, digestion*

PSYCHOLOGICAL CORRESPONDENCE: *Enthusiasm, emotional strength*

ASSOCIATED CRYSTALS BY COLOR: *Golden quartz, bronze*

KEYWORDS: *Originality, opportunity*

THE CRYSTAL

Sunstone is a member of the feldspar family, and is named for its warm shades of gold, reds, and browns that sparkle like the sun. Inclusions of goethite or hematite refract light between the different crystal layers and produce an iridescent effect as the stone is viewed from various angles.

LEGENDARY USES

In ancient Greece, sunstone was considered a magical talisman and to wear it attracted good health and prosperity. It was also thought to promote abundance to all fortunate enough to possess it. Used in the ornamentation of goblets and plates, the stone was also used as an antidote to poison and to enhance personal strength. Believed to be a piece of the sun itself, sunstone was prized by ancient Babylonian magi, who used it to attract the sun god's blessing, and harness solar power.

ATTRIBUTES AND POWERS

Sunstone is one of the best abundance stones around. It not only encourages independence and opportunity, but is inspirational in revealing your true potential, attracting fame and unexpected prosperity. It is an excellent good luck crystal, increasing vitality and bringing you extra optimism and enthusiasm for life. If you have difficulty saying "no," carry sunstone to stop you from always being a compromising angel. Wearing sunstone regularly removes inhibitions and hangups, increases feelings of self-worth, and brings opportunities for leadership and promotion and the chance to really shine.

HOW TO USE

Place seven pieces of sunstone in a sunny place in a spiral starting from the first stone in the center and moving outward in a clockwise direction—leave for seven days to promote abundant luck in your life.

TIGER'S EYE

APPEARANCE/COLOR: *Black with yellow/brown/gold stripes*

CURRENT AVAILABILITY: *Easily obtained*

PHYSIOLOGICAL CORRESPONDENCE: *Eyes, reproductive organs*

PSYCHOLOGICAL CORRESPONDENCE: *Self-worth, creativity*

ASSOCIATED CRYSTALS BY COLOR: *Cat's eye, aragonite*

KEYWORDS: *Trust, realistic goals*

THE CRYSTAL

Tiger's Eye belongs to the so-called "chatoyant" group of quartz. A crocidolite mineral is the cause for its shimmering flashes of light that give the cat's eye effect. The most common form of tiger's eye is black with iron oxide staining that creates the yellow and brown stripes.

LEGENDARY USES

Highly regarded throughout history as a stone of prosperity and good fortune, tiger's eye has been used to protect against curses and to reflect back any evil intentions from others onto themselves. When worn, it was revered and feared as an "all-seeing, all-knowing eye," and was thought to grant the wearer the ability to observe everything, even through closed doors. A popular good luck stone, tiger's eye was also worn by Roman soldiers as an amulet to deflect weapons in battle.

ATTRIBUTES AND POWERS

Tiger's eye enables you to discriminate clearly between what you think you need and what you actually need. As a stone of luck and good fortune wearing tiger's eye will attract a steady flow of abundance to you. It is ideal for anyone setting out in business for the first time and also for engaging in any new enterprise or seeking major career changes in the future. Tiger's eye gives you a realistic "eye" for your own talents and for trying something new. It can be used as a support stone to overcome fears of selling or presenting ideas in important meetings. Carry with you to boost quick thinking, good judgment, and sizing up someone's character.

HOW TO USE

For abundant success in your career, by day, place two pieces of tiger's eye at each end of your desk, and by night, under your pillow, for one lunar cycle.

TOPAZ (IMPERIAL)

APPEARANCE/COLOR: *Light gold*

CURRENT AVAILABILITY: *Available from specialty stores, but expensive*

PHYSIOLOGICAL CORRESPONDENCE: *Cellular system*

PSYCHOLOGICAL CORRESPONDENCE: *Optimism, ambition*

ASSOCIATED CRYSTALS BY COLOR: *Citrine, yellow sapphire*

KEYWORDS: *Charisma, confidence in future plans*

THE CRYSTAL

Topaz can be found as huge, flawless crystals, often faceted into giant gemstones which can weigh thousands of carats. Imperial or golden topaz and the dark pinkish-red and orange-red colors are the most valuable. Topaz is found in locations worldwide, including Russia, Brazil, the USA, and Australia.

LEGENDARY USES

Most scholars now believe that the stone's name derives from the ancient Sanskrit word *topas* or *tapaz*, meaning "fire." To the ancient Egyptians, the stone symbolized Ra, the sun god, giver of life and fertility and it was thought to harness the power of the sun and for the wearer to become almost god-like. The Hindus believed it would protect their homes from fire, and worn above the heart would assure long life, beauty, and intelligence. The ancient Greeks and Romans thought topaz endowed the wearer with great strength and courage, and in medieval Europe it was believed to cure inflammation and stop nosebleeds.

ATTRIBUTES AND POWERS

Wearing imperial topaz boosts your sense of status, empowers you with self-belief, and gives you the personal will and ability to manifest your desires. If you are seeking fame, fortune, or simply looking to be at the top of a career ladder, this is the most beneficial stone you can wear or carry. It can also help overcome limitations, increase charisma, attract helpful people, but still enable you to remain generous and open-hearted toward others. Imperial topaz brings success in all endeavors. All manifestation rituals using this stone clarify your intentions and focuses your thoughts and turn those desires into physical reality.

HOW TO USE

Topaz is highly effective when held or touched when performing all affirmations and the visualization techniques suggested in this book.

TOURMALINE (GREEN)

APPEARANCE/COLOR: *Green*

CURRENT AVAILABILITY: *Widely available*

PHYSIOLOGICAL CORRESPONDENCE: *Nervous system*

PSYCHOLOGICAL CORRESPONDENCE: *Joy, vitality*

ASSOCIATED CRYSTALS BY COLOR: *Jade, aventurine*

KEYWORDS: *Transformation, positive change*

THE CRYSTAL

Tourmaline appears in many different colors, including blue, red, pink, black, and green. This wide color range is due to the varying mineral content within the stone's complicated chemical make-up. For example, magnesium creates blue to brown tourmalines, while lithium colors the stone anything from green to pink. Tourmalines are found in Africa, Russia, the USA, and Myanmar. Green tourmaline, also known as verdelite, like other forms, changes color when viewed from various angles.

LEGENDARY USES

Tourmaline was first brought to Europe by Dutch traders in the 1700s who placed a piece of the crystal on the end of their tobacco pipes to suck up the old ash. The stone became known as the "ash puller" because of its electrostatic power. Heating or rubbing tourmaline causes it to become electrically charged, and is one of its distinguishing qualities.

ATTRIBUTES AND POWERS

Green tourmaline is a stone that not only attracts dust because of its electrostatic charge, but also luck, success, abundance, and prosperity. With its ability to promote creative thinking and problem solving, it is a great crystal to use in grids to help your goals flourish and manifest. The stone is perfect for maintaining steady progress of a new venture, ensuring a project stays on schedule, or just simply keeping yourself working toward an important achievement. The lighter green crystals are best used for manifesting abundant spiritual growth, while darker green tourmaline is the perfect crystal for manifesting abundant ambition, wealth, or general success.

HOW TO USE

Wear or carry with you to attract people, ideas, and opportunities as you travel forward toward your intended current goal.

TURQUOISE

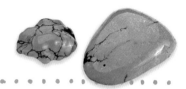

APPEARANCE/COLOR: *Turquoise blue; turquoise green (Tibetan turquoise)*

CURRENT AVAILABILITY: *Widely available*

PHYSIOLOGICAL CORRESPONDENCE: *Immune system*

PSYCHOLOGICAL CORRESPONDENCE: *Self-assurance, creativity*

ASSOCIATED CRYSTALS BY COLOR: *Amazonite, aquamarine*

KEYWORDS: *Responsibility, good decision-making*

THE CRYSTAL

Turquoise is a blend of copper and aluminum phosphates, and its name is said to be derived from the French term *pierre turquoise*, meaning "Turkish stone." This mistakenly referenced the gems brought back by European traders in the medieval period from Turkey whereas the stones they purchased had been mined in Central Asia, not Turkey. Found worldwide, its primary sources today are the USA, China, Tibet, Australia, and northern India.

LEGENDARY USES

Turkish warriors fighting Christian Crusaders wore turquoise to protect themselves in battle. The stone enabled them to overcome their fears, and fight with inner calm and certainty of victory. Emperor Rudolph II's court physician, Anselmus de Boot, wrote in 1609 that turquoise was so highly regarded by men that no man considered his hand to be well adorned unless he wore the stone. Native American shamans would use it as a "universal stone of truth" in rituals. They believed they would become one with the universe when wearing the stone, and it was also used in prophesy and divination work.

ATTRIBUTES AND POWERS

With its ability to clear the mind, invoke deepest wisdom, and genuine self-expression, turquoise is highly beneficial for all forms of self-realization. So for abundant knowledge, truth, and knowing where you are going in life, this is the stone to wear or carry. Not only does it aid in creative problem-solving, but helps stabilize moods, and dissolve self-sabotaging thoughts. Turquoise enhances the ability to see all aspects of ourselves, warts and all, and to integrate these aspects into a cohesive whole. As a manifestation stone, turquoise will empower you with personal truth and a realistic glimpse of how you can make your life what you desire it to be.

HOW TO USE

Place a circle of five stones in the north corner of a home or room for five days, then carry them with you for another five days to work their magic and attract flourishing ideas and plans.

CRYSTALS *for* SUCCESS

· ·

This section covers crystals that are particularly aligned to manifesting the energy of success. Of course, success means many different things to each of us. We can feel successful by growing great tomatoes or show off how successful we are in business or our career by displaying our wealth or status symbols. We can feel success within our hearts and souls because of our spiritual alignment, or simply because we know that "success" is a quality which implies we have achieved a goal.

The word success derives from the Latin word *succedere*, "to come close after." So if you are looking to have a favorable result and want it to come close after, or very soon for whatever reason, these are the crystals that will help to promote personal success in whatever you do, particularly in the realm of business, career, and creative achievement. These stones also attract opportunities and people to you, both of which herald new pathways to manifesting specific or intentional goals.

ALBITE

APPEARANCE/COLOR: *White or translucent with bluish tinge*

CURRENT AVAILABILITY: *Readily available*

PHYSIOLOGICAL CORRESPONDENCE: *Eyes, blood*

PSYCHOLOGICAL CORRESPONDENCE: *Confidence, personal freedom*

ASSOCIATED CRYSTALS BY COLOR: *Celestite, clear calcite*

KEYWORDS: *Making changes for a successful life*

THE CRYSTAL

Albite is a feldspar mineral which occurs in granitic (granite-like rock) and pegmatite (intrusive igneous rock) masses. The crystal takes the form of flat blades or tall prismatic crystals. Fine examples of albite are found in Canada, the Swiss Alps, Afghanistan, and Virginia, USA.

LEGENDARY USES

There are no legends surrounding albite, except the stone often known as the rainbow moonstone is a cut and polished form of this gemstone. Rainbow moonstone was a sacred stone of ancient India. According to earliest traditions, the stone had been set in the forehead of the four-handed god of the moon. With its association with the lunar god, and its prismatic colors, which change like the waxing and waning of the moon, it was thus given the name moonstone.

ATTRIBUTES AND POWERS

Known as a stone of resolute action, albite enhances clear thinking and improves one's ability to cooperate with tact and diplomacy. The stone is also said to give the wearer courage and confidence when confronting the unknown. With its powerful ability to encourage personal growth, freedom, and the desire for change, it is a superb stone to help you manifest your goals. Albite promotes acting on ideas, and provides insight into how to work out your plans for the future. Enhancing personal power, albite enables you to prosper in your chosen field, or to dramatically attract new opportunities.

HOW TO USE

Place in the north corner of your business or home to enhance career and personal success.

AMETRINE

APPEARANCE/COLOR: *Purple and yellow*

CURRENT AVAILABILITY: *Available, but only from one mine so can be expensive*

PHYSIOLOGICAL CORRESPONDENCE: *Nervous system*

PSYCHOLOGICAL CORRESPONDENCE: *Perception, creativity*

ASSOCIATED CRYSTALS BY COLOR: *Amethyst, citrine*

KEYWORDS: *Stimulates ideas and positive transformation*

THE CRYSTAL

Ametrine is a naturally occurring variety of quartz. It is a mix of amethyst and citrine which create zones of purple and yellow or orange. Ametrine is currently mined only in Bolivia, although some deposits have been found in Brazil and India.

LEGENDARY USES

Although ametrine was only brought to the gem market in the 1970s, a legend dating from the 18th century tells how this stone was the key to a terrible tragedy. A Spanish conquistador named Don Felipe is said to have married a Bolivian princess. The mine, named in her honor, was given to him as part of her dowry. When it was time for Felipe to return to Spain with his bride, her family turned on the couple in anger and murdered the young princess. The dual-colored gem has since then been said to represent the girl's loyalty to both her husband and to her people.

ATTRIBUTES AND POWERS

This duality legend enables us to understand the double power of ametrine. It promotes both the spiritual awakening and clarity of amethyst, enabling us to connect to the universe and manifest successful goals, coupled with the power of citrine, the attractor of abundance, opportunity, and chances. Ametrine enhances all intellectual skills and pursuits and attracts fortunate communication and successful people to guide you. It clarifies all problems, aids decision-making, and enables you to make creative solutions. A powerful stone for manifesting success in all you do, its power is amplified when placed in a grid with amethyst and citrine stones as described below.

HOW TO USE

Place one piece of ametrine in the center of a four-cardinal-points grid. To the east and west place citrine, and to the north and south place amethyst to create a matrix for success.

APATITE (BLUE)

APPEARANCE/COLOR: *Blue, and other colors*

CURRENT AVAILABILITY: *Widely available*

PHYSIOLOGICAL CORRESPONDENCE: *Metabolism, cartilage, bones*

PSYCHOLOGICAL CORRESPONDENCE: *Motivation, sociability*

ASSOCIATED CRYSTALS BY COLOR: *Blue lace agate, larimar*

KEYWORDS: *Uplifts and clears the way for success*

THE CRYSTAL

The name apatite derives from the Greek word meaning "deception." Occurring in transparent, translucent, and opaque forms, apatite ranges in color from white to brown to green to yellow. Its crystal form is hexagonal and glassy in appearance. Found worldwide, its most important sources are Brazil, Myanmar, and Mexico.

LEGENDARY USES

Because apatite is a recently discovered mineral, there are no legends surrounding it, but recent crystal healers have been amazed by its ability to stimulate the third-eye chakra, reviving objective perception and a new perspective of the world around us. In this way it helps us to balance ideas, and understand how we are reacting to, or "seeing" the world before us. This stone helps us to interpret visual cues but also our inner thoughts become more healthy and vibrant as negativity is dispelled. Apatite also balances the throat chakra, so that we can communicate those ideas and get results.

ATTRIBUTES AND POWERS

Apatite enhances all psychic abilities and can be used in meditation to bring a true willingness to let go of people, objects, and situations that have become meaningless in one's life. Apatite is often known as a "humanitarian" stone because it allows you to accept others for who they are and give your love freely and unconditionally, but also have belief and trust in exactly what it is that will bring you the success you deserve. Known for its positive use of personal power to achieve goals, it clears confusion, apathy or negativity, and stimulates personal growth, motivation, independence, and ambition.

HOW TO USE

Place in the northeast corner of your home to enhance all communication channels for positive results.

ARAGONITE

APPEARANCE/COLOR: *White, yellow, gold, brown, green*

CURRENT AVAILABILITY: *Widely available*

PHYSIOLOGICAL CORRESPONDENCE: *Nervous and immune systems*

PSYCHOLOGICAL CORRESPONDENCE: *Patience, acceptance, self-discipline*

ASSOCIATED CRYSTALS BY COLOR: *Opal, smoky quartz*

KEYWORDS: *Grounding, insight, strength, support*

THE CRYSTAL

Aragonite usually appears as small clusters of spikes, usually brown, cream, or white. Aragonite is one of the main components of pearls and coral. The iridescent surface of mother-of-pearl, the inner part of the shell that guards the pearl, is a layer of aragonite secreted by mollusks.

LEGENDARY USES

Aragonite may not be well known as a crystal by its own name, but as it is the prime component of the iridescent surface of pearl it probably has more legendary fame than many other crystals worldwide. To the ancient Greeks, pearls were tears of joy that Aphrodite shed when she was born from the sea foam. Mesopotamian mythology also recounts similar tales of how pearls were crystallized tears. In some early Persian legends pearls were thought to be solidified drops of the moon, while the oysters that give birth to the pearls were lured to the sea by the moon itself.

ATTRIBUTES AND POWERS

Aragonite is thought to relieve geopathic stress and open blocked ley lines on the Earth's surface. When placed in specific locations around the home the stone creates balance and harmony. Mentally, aragonite aids concentration and promotes practical ability. Wearing aragonite also brings great strength of mind, enabling you to make choices based on logic and reason rather than being led astray by emotion. As a stone of manifestation, it invokes pragmatic energy, enabling you to delegate to the right people to achieve successful results. A practical stone, it keeps your feet firmly on the ground and offers the chance to spot and seize potential opportunities.

HOW TO USE

Place on your desk or in the southeast corner of your office or workplace to attract achievement.

AZURITE

APPEARANCE/COLOR: *Deep blue*

CURRENT AVAILABILITY: *Easily obtained*

PHYSIOLOGICAL CORRESPONDENCE: *Joints, spine, teeth, skin*

PSYCHOLOGICAL CORRESPONDENCE: *Insight, stress-relief*

ASSOCIATED CRYSTALS BY COLOR: *Lapis lazuli, sodalite*

KEYWORDS: *Enlightened thinking, self-expression*

THE CRYSTAL

Azurite is a soft stone, named for its deep azure-blue color. It is a copper carbonate mineral found in the oxidized portions of copper ore. The saturated color ranges from bright to deep blue into shades of indigo, and may contain streaks of light blue.

LEGENDARY USES

Thought to be a heavenly stone by the ancient Chinese, azurite was said to open celestial gateways which led you to the lands of the gods. Revered by Greeks and Romans, it was made into elixirs for visionary insight and healing power. For the Mayans, azurite inspired spiritual knowledge and telepathic powers, while Native American shamans used the stone in rituals to contact their Spirit Guides. Called *caeruleum*, meaning "pertaining to the sky or the sea," by the ancient Greeks, because of its brilliant blue color, azurite was ground and used as a dye for paints and fabrics.

ATTRIBUTES AND POWERS

Expanding your awareness, azurite enables you to really know what it is you are hoping to manifest. It is particularly helpful in dissolving old or unnecessary belief systems, which may be holding you back from your true quest. Azurite asks you to question your desires. Are they built on other people's expectations or your own? Can you truly express yourself, or are you blocked by old habits, doubts, or fears? The deep azure blue of the stone asks you to look deep within yourself, as if looking into the depths of the sea and finding that beneath all the higher swimming sharks, is another world of deep sea illumination. Discovering this place will bring you the kind of success you may not have ever imagined.

HOW TO USE

As a "rubbing" stone, azurite likes to be touched to release its energies, so wear or carry azurite and touch or gently rub it often to aid in your quest for achievement.

AGATE (BLUE LACE)

APPEARANCE/COLOR: *Pale blue and darker colored veins*

CURRENT AVAILABILITY: *Widely available*

PHYSIOLOGICAL CORRESPONDENCE: *Throat, thyroid, lymph glands*

PSYCHOLOGICAL CORRESPONDENCE: *Self-expression*

ASSOCIATED CRYSTALS BY COLOR: *Celestite, aquamarine*

KEYWORDS: *Communication, contacts, successful mentors*

THE CRYSTAL

Blue lace agate is a form of chalcedony, a mineral of the quartz family. Its "lace" effect is due to mineral inclusions, which create wavy or lacy layers of light blue, white, and even brown threads of color running through the stone. Like other agates, it is found in the USA, Brazil, Mexico, India, and Australia.

LEGENDARY USES

Ancient Romans valued blue varieties of agate for their reputed medicinal and talismanic properties. Powdered and mixed with water, it was said to counteract serpents' venom. Wearing the stone was believed to be a cure for insomnia and was thought to invoke pleasant dreams. Medieval legends claim agate had the power to protect children from falling, endow its wearer with strength, courage, and the ability to dissolve all fears. Renaissance philosopher and writer, Gerolamo Cardano, told of how a blue agate had helped him to succeed in philosophical debates, tempering his moods, and making him more considerate in his dealings.

ATTRIBUTES AND POWERS

Blue lace agate promotes a sense of reality and aids in pragmatic thinking. Enhancing discernment and discretion, it will help you to decide which thoughts to share and which to keep to yourself. The stone also inspires loyalty and trustworthiness from others, so is often referred to as the "stone of the diplomat." It is the perfect companion to carry with you when dealing with others to avoid angry words or misunderstandings, and to boost all-round positive communication.

HOW TO USE

Wear as jewelry or carry with you whenever you need to speak the truth with diplomatic grace and attract useful mentors.

CARNELIAN

APPEARANCE/COLOR: *Red, orange*

CURRENT AVAILABILITY: *Common*

PHYSIOLOGICAL CORRESPONDENCE: *Kidneys*

PSYCHOLOGICAL CORRESPONDENCE: *Trust, determination*

ASSOCIATED CRYSTALS BY COLOR: *Fire agate, amber*

KEYWORDS: *Empowerment, focus, luck*

THE CRYSTAL

Carnelian is an orange-colored variety of chalcedony, and thus a silica mineral which is part of the quartz family. It can appear as anything from pale orange to a deep rusty brown. The best colors for manifestation work are orange or red.

LEGENDARY USES

Known as the "setting sun stone" by the ancient Egyptians, it was identified with female energy, and associated with the menstrual blood of the mother goddess, Isis. Although carnelian is traditionally worn to enhance passion, love, and desire, it was also a stone carried by Mesopotamian warriors to protect them in battle. Ancient Persians used carnelian to stop bleeding, while medieval Hebrew peoples believed it would prevent them from catching the plague. The Greeks and Romans used carnelian for signet rings and amulets. These were engraved with symbols of the planets or auspicious gods, such as Zeus or Minerva.

ATTRIBUTES AND POWERS

Although carnelian is essential in promoting love and passion, it is also a highly important stone for success, good luck, and prosperity. Bestowing terrific powers of concentration, it can also help you overcome a fear of public speaking. To promote self-worth, carnelian can be worn or carried daily and it is a great stone to boost any form of career success. This stone also protects against envy, rage, and resentment and encourages a love of life. Like many red stones, carnelian is a stimulant, and so a powerful talisman for manifesting success in any money-making venture.

HOW TO USE

Invite prosperity and success into your workplace by placing carnelian near the front door or main entrance.

CELESTITE

APPEARANCE/COLOR: *Pale blue*

CURRENT AVAILABILITY: *Widely available but expensive*

PHYSIOLOGICAL CORRESPONDENCE: *Muscles, cellular structure*

PSYCHOLOGICAL CORRESPONDENCE: *Deeper self-awareness, higher consciousness*

ASSOCIATED CRYSTALS BY COLOR: *Blue lace agate, angelite*

KEYWORDS: *Fine-tuned perception, good fortune*

THE CRYSTAL

Composed of the mineral strontium sulcate, celestite is found in areas where long-term weathering has begun to break up limestone and sandstone rock masses. Celestite is found worldwide, but the finest examples come from the USA, Madagascar, and Spain.

LEGENDARY USES

The name derives from the Latin *caelestis,* meaning "celestial" or "heavenly." Although few legends are associated with this stone, it has become an important tourist attraction in a limestone cave located in Put-in-Bay, on South Bass Island in Lake Erie, Ohio. Apparently, in 1887, Gustav Heineman emigrated from Baden-Baden in Germany to Put-in-Bay, where he established a winery. In 1897 he dug a well beneath his winery and discovered a cave covered with crystals of celestine. Mr. Heineman turned the property into a tourist attraction, and luckily, his winery survived the Prohibition era, thanks to the tourist revenue. The cave's remarkable celestine crystals—up to 3 feet (1 m) wide—can still be viewed.

ATTRIBUTES AND POWERS

Celestite attracts luck and success, just as Mr. Heineman's cave fortuitously saw him through Prohibition. It also calms tempers, gives one strength of purpose and a deep belief in the workings of the universe. As a stone for manifesting success it gives you the power to know what it is you truly seek and the ability to follow your intuition. Celestite also bestows on you a sense of having a "guardian angel" at your side, so that you can trust in your decisions and perceive the world and your place in it from an objective perspective. Celestite also aids mental clarity as it clears and sharpens the mind.

HOW TO USE

Place a small geode cluster of this lovely blue stone in the south corner of your home to keep you sharp and alert.

CHALCEDONY

APPEARANCE/COLOR: *Blue, grayish-white*

CURRENT AVAILABILITY: *Common*

PHYSIOLOGICAL CORRESPONDENCE: *Gallbladder, spleen, lactation*

PSYCHOLOGICAL CORRESPONDENCE: *Generosity, benevolence*

ASSOCIATED CRYSTALS BY COLOR: *Moonstone, white jade*

KEYWORDS: *Goodwill, a sense of solidarity and agreement*

THE CRYSTAL

Sometimes written as "calcedony," the stone is a fine-grained form of silica mineral quartz. It has a waxy luster and appears in a great variety of colors. Named after the ancient seaport of Chalcedon in Asia Minor, archeologists have found Babylonian and Assyrian chalcedony cylinder-seals dating from 750 BCE.

LEGENDARY USES

In Roman times, chalcedony was often engraved with mystical symbols to assist in successful lawsuits and disputes. The great Roman orator Cicero is said to have worn a pendant of blue chalcedony, and today it is still known as the "speaker's stone." In Renaissance magic, the stone was often processed and prescribed as an elixir by sorcerers, alchemists, and apothecaries to banish unwanted illusions, nightmares, and fantasies.

Considered a sacred stone by Native American peoples, it was said to be used to channel oracular or prophetic information from the spirit world.

ATTRIBUTES AND POWERS

Chalcedony is a nurturing stone of calmness and composure, opening the mind to new ideas, and enhancing receptivity and responsiveness. Wearing the stone makes you to be more benevolent, enhances your generosity, and bestows on you an enthusiastic outlook on life. With clarity and emotional honesty, it allows you to see the truth of any situation. As the "speaker's stone" it promotes great listening and speaking skills, stimulating your mind and making new languages easier to learn or understand.

HOW TO USE

Wear or carry blue chalcedony when you want to make a great impression on someone and nail a future achievement.

CHRYSOPRASE

APPEARANCE/COLOR: *Apple green*

CURRENT AVAILABILITY: *Common*

PHYSIOLOGICAL CORRESPONDENCE: *Hormones, digestive system*

PSYCHOLOGICAL CORRESPONDENCE: *Objectivity, contentment*

ASSOCIATED CRYSTALS BY COLOR: *Green calcite, green sapphire*

KEYWORDS: *Acceptance of self and others, promotes creativity*

THE CRYSTAL

Chrysoprase is a name deriving from the Greek words *chrysos*, meaning "gold," and *prasinon*, meaning "green." Sometimes referred to as the "mother of jade," chrysoprase is a beautiful opalescent apple-green form of chalcedony.

LEGENDARY USES

It is said that the ancient Greeks may have given this stone its name due to the presence of the golden drops it appears to contain. Thought to be magical, it was left outside during the full moon in order to invoke prosperity, good health, and a happy marriage. In Mesopotamia, chrysoprase was believed to be the sacred flame of the indigenous goddess, Ninsun or Nammu, and it is currently being revived as an altar stone for those who practice Mother Goddess worship.

ATTRIBUTES AND POWERS

Chrysoprase has been one of the major stones used to banish greed, selfishness, and carelessness, and to enhance happiness, action, progress, and adventure. The stone is used to promote success for new enterprises and to bestow tolerance, creative thinking, and genuine belief in your goals. Carry or wear chrysoprase to attract prosperity and money, but also as a protection against negative thoughts from others. The stone gives you confidence and business acumen, enhances charisma, and inspires creative thinking. It also gives you the motivation and ambition for all you seek.

HOW TO USE

Place chrysoprase in each of the cardinal compass point corners of your home to boost all forms of prosperity.

DIOPTASE

APPEARANCE/COLOR: *Deep blue-green*

CURRENT AVAILABILITY: *Rare*

PHYSIOLOGICAL CORRESPONDENCE: *Cellular system, heart, and liver*

PSYCHOLOGICAL CORRESPONDENCE: *Emotional healing*

ASSOCIATED CRYSTALS BY COLOR: *Atacamite, chrysocolla*

KEYWORDS: *Fulfilling potential, positive forward-thinking*

THE CRYSTAL

Dioptase is very fragile due to its brittle, prismatic structure, and specimens must be handled with great care. The stone is an intense emerald-green to bluish-green copper silicate mineral found only in desert areas such as those of Kazahkstan, Arizona, Namibia, and Argentina.

LEGENDARY USES

In the 18th century, copper miners in Kazakhstan thought they had discovered the emerald deposit of their dreams when they found thousands of emerald-green transparent crystals embedded in quartz veins running through limestone cavities. The crystals were eventually dispatched to Moscow for analysis. But the mineral's inferior hardness of 5, compared with emerald's greater hardness of 8, revealed they were not emeralds but a new mineral which, in 1797, was named dioptase from the Greek *dio*, meaning "through," and *optos*, meaning "visible."

ATTRIBUTES AND POWERS

These days crystal healers use dioptase to promote a high level of spiritual awareness. However, for manifestation purposes, it is an empowering stone. When worn it gives you charisma, and delights you with positive thinking and energy. The stone also brings your hidden potential to light, and enables you to unleash your talents and work with your resources. Filtering out "neediness" from desire, it dissolves vulnerability, banishes resentment and greed, and alleviates any sense of betrayal and mistrust. A stone that can bring you success in everything you intend to do, it clears the mind of self-reproach and lack of self-belief and replaces it with trust and motivation.

HOW TO USE

Place five pieces of dioptase in the shape of a pentagram, light a green candle in the center, and ask the universe to bring you success for your chosen goal.

FLUORITE

APPEARANCE/COLOR: *Available in a range of colors*

CURRENT AVAILABILITY: *Common*

PHYSIOLOGICAL CORRESPONDENCE: *Teeth, bones, arthritis*

PSYCHOLOGICAL CORRESPONDENCE: *Progress, promotes self-confidence, focus*

ASSOCIATED CRYSTALS BY COLOR: *Phenacite, white opal*

KEYWORDS: *Awareness, protection, clarity*

THE CRYSTAL

Much loved by mineralogists and healers alike, fluorite crystals are vibrant, luminous, soft, and glassy, with an ordered internal structure. Under ultraviolet light many specimens reveal fluorescence, the phenomenon itself taking its name from fluorite.

LEGENDARY USES

Fluorite is believed to have been used by the ancient Egyptians for carving scarabs and statues of the gods. The Chinese were known to use fluorite as a substitute for their highly prized stone, jade (see page 92). The Romans treasured their "fluorospar" drinking cups, not only for the exquisite colors of this beautiful stone, but for the curious flavor the stone gave to their wine. The Roman author Pliny the Elder speaks of at least one Roman noble who enjoyed chewing the edge of his vessel to get more of the flavor out of the stone.

ATTRIBUTES AND POWERS

Fluorite is one of the most favored of success stones. It not only keeps negative energy at bay, but helps you to see the truth about people around you. Wearing fluorite makes you aware of external influences that could be harmful, and simultaneously protects you from psychic manipulation by others. It is also highly effective as a protection against geopathic stress and other electromagnetic negativity in the environment. Enhancing purity of thought, fluorite maintains balance and order while dissolving any manipulation by rivals or envious onlookers.

HOW TO USE

Keep a stone on your desk at work to dispel negative energy, sly tricksters, or those who might lead you away from your success story.

OPAL (FIRE)

APPEARANCE/COLOR: *Orange/red*

CURRENT AVAILABILITY: *Common, but gem opals are expensive*

PHYSIOLOGICAL CORRESPONDENCE: *Abdomen, intestines, adrenal glands*

PSYCHOLOGICAL CORRESPONDENCE: *Progress, letting go of the past*

ASSOCIATED CRYSTALS BY COLOR: *Carnelian, red sardonyx*

KEYWORDS: *Potent success, business booster*

THE CRYSTAL

Opal is formed from silica spheres bonded together with water and additional silica. Because it has no crystalline structure, it is considered to be a mineraloid rather than a mineral. Fire opal is a transparent to translucent stone most commonly mined in Mexico.

LEGENDARY USES

For the Aztecs the fire opal bestowed their leader with ferocious energy and invincibility. Known as the "bird of paradise stone" it was thought to embody the power of their creator god, Quetzalcoatl. It could also activate new beginnings, but also see the destruction of rivals. While the Aztecs may have been more interested in its warring powers, the Egyptians and Babylonians honored the opal as a powerful healing gem. The ancient Romans thought the stone embodied all the other gemstones because of its colors, and since the medieval period it has been worn to improve sight or bestow good luck on the wearer.

ATTRIBUTES AND POWERS

Fire opal boosts personal power and attracts good business to you. Aligned to the creative energy of the universe, it is the ideal stone for boosting all creative and marketing projects. Fire opals not only manifest money to those who seek it, but also facilitates change, and allows you to make quick progress. It makes an excellent guiding stone should you wish to be independent and live by your own rules. It is also the stone to keep with you if you want to make your mark in life. Fire opals protect you against malevolent thoughts from others and empower with you with the will to go out and get what you truly desire.

HOW TO USE

Wear or carry fire opal to become totally optimistic, socially outgoing, and sure of your success.

HESSONITE

APPEARANCE/COLOR: *Orange to rich dark brown, cinnamon*

CURRENT AVAILABILITY: *Relatively rare*

PHYSIOLOGICAL CORRESPONDENCE: *Nervous system*

PSYCHOLOGICAL CORRESPONDENCE: *Emotional ease*

ASSOCIATED CRYSTALS BY COLOR: *Cinnabar, red jasper*

KEYWORDS: *Successful enterprises, good fortune*

THE CRYSTAL

Hessonite is also called the cinnamon stone, not only for its color, but because it originates in Sri Lanka, once the greatest spice trader with the West. A gem variety of garnet, its beauty is renowned. Mineralogists named this variety of garnet from the Greek word *hesson*, meaning "inferior," because its structure is less dense than other garnets.

LEGENDARY USES

Hessonite garnet is a major crystal used in the Vedic astrological tradition. The nine planetary gemstones, which correspond to and therefore "carry" the energy of the planet concerned, are: ruby, diamond, pearl, red coral, blue sapphire, cat's eye, yellow sapphire, emerald, and hessonite garnet. Hessonite, known in Sanskrit as *gomeda* ("cow fat"), is the stone associated with Rahu, which, in the Hindu tradition, is the moon's ascending node. A negatively placed Rahu in an astrological birth chart signifies that the individual is deluded by insatiable worldly desires and sensual gratification! Luckily, wearing or carrying hessonite dissolves its own negative energy.

ATTRIBUTES AND POWERS

Vedic (Hindu) astrologers believe that wearing a hessonite garnet of at least two carats can promote success, wealth, and recognition. And, since ancient times, Hessonite is thought to bestow the wearer with longevity and to attract good fortune. It is a fabulous stone for attracting success, particularly in any independent or newly formed business. It also enhances creative thinking, or projects for finding a niche in the market. With this stone you can be sure of attracting the right kind of mentors to you, and for being in the right place at the right time to seize any opportunity.

HOW TO USE

Wear or carry hessonite to inspire you wherever you go, and to attract great results in business.

HOWLITE

APPEARANCE/COLOR: *White, green, mottled gray*

CURRENT AVAILABILITY: *Common*

PHYSIOLOGICAL CORRESPONDENCE: *Nervous system*

PSYCHOLOGICAL CORRESPONDENCE: *Creative potential*

ASSOCIATED CRYSTALS BY COLOR: *White aragonite, petalite*

KEYWORDS: *Charisma and self-confidence*

THE CRYSTAL

Howlite is a borate mineral, and is mostly found in California as well as Mexico, Russia, and Turkey. Natural howlite is always white or gray, and, undyed, its porcelain-like glow is attractive. However, because of its highly porous strucure, it is often dyed to resemble other stones.

LEGENDARY USES

There is no known legends surrounding this stone. It wasn't discovered until the 19th century, in Nova Scotia, by Canadian mineralogist Henry How, for whom the stone was named. The strange, smooth stone is found in its original state in large cauliflower-like masses. Its natural color is white with gray and black veins. Dyed with rich hues it can resemble turquoise, lapis lazuli, or even red coral.

ATTRIBUTES AND POWERS

Howlite is known for its strong associations with self-awareness, creativity, and improving one's emotional well-being. Wearing the stone enhances charisma, character and strengthens one's self-confidence and self-love. For manifesting success, it allows you to work with your talents and potentials, rather than assume you must do as others do. Howlite dispels selfish or idealistic dreams, and asks you to look inside yourself for the truth. When used in grids or layouts to increase business success, it will help you communicate with discretion, without provoking confrontations.

HOW TO USE

Place five pieces of white howlite in a pentagram shape in the northeast corner of your home or desk. Leave for five days and nights to boost your communication powers.

IOLITE

APPEARANCE/COLOR: *Violet, blue, gray, yellow*

CURRENT AVAILABILITY: *Available from specialty stores*

PHYSIOLOGICAL CORRESPONDENCE: *Liver, respiratory system*

PSYCHOLOGICAL CORRESPONDENCE: *Clarity, focus*

ASSOCIATED CRYSTALS BY COLOR: *Blue calcite, sodalite*

KEYWORDS: *Freedom from the chains of expectation*

THE CRYSTAL

Iolite appears as violet-blue or indigo but, looked at from a different angle, it may change to a yellow or gray, a phenomenon known as pleochroism. The name iolite comes from the Greek word *ios*, meaning violet, and this stone is also sometimes knows as "water sapphire."

LEGENDARY USES

It is believed that iolite may be the true stone of the Vikings, used by Leif Eriksson and other explorers when trying to discover the New World. Far away from the coastline they used thin pieces of iolite to navigate and determine their direction, particularly during cloud cover, to work out their position. Looking through an iolite lens, they could determine the exact position of the sun and navigate safely to the New World. Light scattered by water molecules (i.e. clouds, fog, or rain) is polarized. These early navigators worked out that direction of the polarization is at right angles to a line to the sun, even when the sun is obscured by dense fog or lies just below the horizon.

ATTRIBUTES AND POWERS

Iolite is a great stone to restore any lack of confidence so you can brazen forth on the road to success. Wearing or carrying the stone will strengthen your resolve to take on any additional responsibility, enhancing endurance in any adverse situations. If you fee that luck hasn't been on your side, or that you're cursed with negative people or situations, iolite restores a sense of perspective. It also turns chaos to order, and promotes a calm, positive state of mind. Instilling belief and strong decision-making abilities, it also enables you to have a clearer perspective on what success really means to you. As a manifestation stone, Iolite activates creative self-expression, and can bring you fantastic ideas that may be radical or unconventional, but at the same time, trendsetting.

HOW TO USE

Wear or carry iolite to boost self-expression and innovative ideas.

IRON PYRITE

APPEARANCE/COLOR: *Gold, brown*

CURRENT AVAILABILITY: *Common*

PHYSIOLOGICAL CORRESPONDENCE: *Bloodstream, digestive system*

PSYCHOLOGICAL CORRESPONDENCE: *Self-worth, confidence*

ASSOCIATED CRYSTALS BY COLOR: *Goldstone, yellow jasper*

KEYWORDS: *Willpower, dynamic action*

THE CRYSTAL

Derived from the Greek word *pyr*, meaning "fire," iron pyrite was named for its ability to emit sparks when pieces were struck against each other. An iron sulphide mineral, pyrite is commonly found around the world as a constituent of metamorphic rock.

LEGENDARY USES

Known more commonly as "fool's gold," the glittering rock was mistaken by naïve gold prospectors as real gold. Dishonest mine-owners added it to their mines, convincing people to dig and walk away with nothing more than fool's gold. Pyrite is harder and more brittle than real gold, and it can't be scratched with a fingernail or knife. In medieval Germany it was known as "cat's gold" and throughout Europe it has been favored as a decorative stone, carved to make shoe buckles, rings, snuff boxes, and other items of ornament. In France it is still known as *pierre de santé*, meaning "stone of health," due to its positive healing powers.

ATTRIBUTES AND POWERS

As sparkling as the stone itself appears, when worn or carried, pyrite bestows you with vitality, will, and dynamic action. This is a crystal that will enable you to tap into your talents, and stimulate success-making ideas. Enhancing confidence and a determination to carry things through to completion, pyrite can be used to manifest all forms of success, from career to wealth, success in love, to improving health. The stone encourages leadership qualities and is a great ally if you're working toward some kind of promotion. As a truth stone, pyrite promotes clarity and insight, encouraging you to overcome doubt and take action, and be more dynamic and confident.

HOW TO USE

Lay a line of ten pieces of pyrite from one end of a south-facing window ledge to the other to draw on the energy of the sun, and to invoke its power of dynamic action. Leave for one lunar cycle.

JADE (RED)

APPEARANCE/COLOR: *Red*

CURRENT AVAILABILITY: *Common*

PHYSIOLOGICAL CORRESPONDENCE: *Sex organs*

PSYCHOLOGICAL CORRESPONDENCE: *Passion, motivation*

ASSOCIATED CRYSTALS BY COLOR: *Garnet, ruby*

KEYWORDS: *Getting what you desire*

THE CRYSTAL

Red jade is a variety of jadeite, one of two distinctly different minerals that share the name jade (see page 92). Jadeite is hard and lustrous, rarer than the softer form, nephrite, and usually more expensive.

LEGENDARY USES

Jade has been used since ancient times in the Far East as a stone to boost and enhance all forms of success in business and in love. However, red jade corresponds to the color of passion, courage, and achievement. The third-century BCE Emperor Qin Shi Huang decorated many of his palace chambers with red jade, believing that would not only enhance his passionate desires, but bring him great wealth, success in war, and many heirs.

ATTRIBUTES AND POWERS

Red jade is a stone which is said to enhance the energy of the warrior. It is a talisman of individual power, dispelling all fear, worry, or doubt. Wearing or carrying the stone prevents you from holding back and urges you to take action. A stone of physical vitality, strength and passion, it stimulates and vitalizes your physical energy, while stabilizing your state of mind. Red jade promotes passionate ideas, and attracts success, but also makes tasks less complex and easier to deal with simply because you have the courage of your convictions to take control of any event. Dark red crystals embody strong, deep feelings, serious thinking, and cool passion.

HOW TO USE

Wear or carry red jade to attract passionate mentors, ideas, and engineer situations where you can truly "shine."

JASPER (YELLOW)

APPEARANCE/COLOR: *Yellow*

CURRENT AVAILABILITY: *Common*

PHYSIOLOGICAL CORRESPONDENCE: *Digestive system*

PSYCHOLOGICAL CORRESPONDENCE: *Intellectual acumen*

ASSOCIATED CRYSTALS BY COLOR: *Yellow jade, yellow moonstone*

KEYWORDS: *Successful outcome, achievement*

THE CRYSTAL

Found worldwide, yellow jasper is a variety of quartz. The presence of iron in its structure gives it a tawny yellow color and it often contains other minerals that create rich patterns and veining, as in the variety known as spider jasper.

LEGENDARY USES

Yellow jasper was historically revered as a talisman of protection and discernment, and has been used by priests, shamans, and magicians to aid and protect them when venturing into the metaphysical world. To the native North American peoples, spider jasper (a variety containing earthy white or dark brown spiderweb markings) is believed to contain the power of the wise Grandmother Spider. The Grandmother Spider created people from four different-colored clays as the four nations of the Earth, then led them out from the darkness where Grandfather Sun breathed life into them.

ATTRIBUTES AND POWERS

Wearing yellow or spider jasper builds self-confidence and enthusiasm, and channels positive energy to attract others to you. For forming good contacts, and making a success in business, carry a piece of yellow jasper to improve all communication channels. It also promotes inner strength and mental clarity, and its stabilizing energy keeps you logical and realistic in times of stress. Yellow jasper also gives you the tenacity and perseverance to overcome any obstacles and to move defiantly toward any achievement. A crystal of the intellect, the stone is an excellent crystal for the workplace to encourage the completion of tasks that may have been put on the backburner.

HOW TO USE

Place one piece of yellow jasper in the north corner of your home, and a piece of spider jasper in the south to boost all pathways to fame or career achievement.

LEPIDOLITE

APPEARANCE/COLOR: *Purple, pink*

CURRENT AVAILABILITY: *Widely available*

PHYSIOLOGICAL CORRESPONDENCE: *Connective tissues*

PSYCHOLOGICAL CORRESPONDENCE: *Change, transition*

ASSOCIATED CRYSTALS BY COLOR: *Purple sapphire, chariote*

KEYWORDS: *Self-respect, self-reliance*

THE CRYSTAL

A type of mica, lepidolite often occurs in sparkling masses surrounding pink tourmaline stones. Rich in lithium, the stone can be lavender, purple, and pink, sparkling with a pinkish glow in its polished form.

LEGENDARY USES

The name derives from the Greek word *lepidos*, meaning "scale," due to the scaly constituents that surround it. As a recently newly discovered stone for the New Age movement there is no current legendary information about lepidolite.

ATTRIBUTES AND POWERS

Believed to calm the mind and remove negativity, lepidolite is a great stone for restoring self-value. A stone of acceptance and trust, it provides the wearer with a sense that they can now let go of the past and move into a new phase or new beginning in their life. When working with this stone, all transitions become positive ones, and as a stone of manifesting success, lepidolite attracts the right kind of change. Activating dynamic and yet disciplined energy, you will soon realize that your long-term goals are in sight. Also with its ability to enhance an independent spirit, the stone not only helps to attract supportive friends, contacts, and colleagues, but brings you a wealth of opportunities to succeed.

HOW TO USE

Place in the northwest area of your home or office to attract the right kind of people and/or ideas to help you succeed.

MOLDAVITE

APPEARANCE/COLOR: *Dark green*

CURRENT AVAILABILITY: *Expensive and increasingly rare*

PHYSIOLOGICAL CORRESPONDENCE: *Holistic*

PSYCHOLOGICAL CORRESPONDENCE: *Deep awareness of self*

ASSOCIATED CRYSTALS BY COLOR: *Malachite, green tourmaline*

KEYWORDS: *Transformative power, good fortune*

THE CRYSTAL

Moldavite is a form of tektite, a crystal structure believed to be extraterrestrial because it is usually found where meteorites impacted the Earth millions of years ago. Moldavite is specific to such an event which occurred in what is now southern Germany, and is only found in the region of the River Moldau where it flows through southern Germany and Czechoslovakia. Translucent dull-green moldavite is unlike other tektites, which are usually a slimy brown.

LEGENDARY USES

Found in archeological sites in central Europe dating back to the Stone Age, moldavite was used not only for arrowheads and cutting tools but as an amulet of good fortune, fertility, and protection. In medieval European folklore, moldavite was given as a betrothal gift to bring harmony to the married couple.

ATTRIBUTES AND POWERS

Carrying or wearing moldavite strengthens your ability to see the "cosmic" viewpoint rather than the narrow, rigid, earthbound one. Because of its intense vibration, the stone links you to higher planes of consciousness and, some say, extraterrestrials, enhancing your intuitive and universal connection. On a more practical note, moldavite counteracts cynicism and enables you to see success on many levels. It is a stone of good fortune, and solves money worries by providing solutions not previously considered. This unconventional stone inspires unexpected solutions and new directions to achieve one's dreams.

HOW TO USE

Carry or wear moldavite to keep you in tune with the universal energy flow and to knows what kind of success you truly seek.

RHYOLITE

APPEARANCE/COLOR: *Mottled green and brown*

CURRENT AVAILABILITY: *Common*

PHYSIOLOGICAL CORRESPONDENCE: *Skin*

PSYCHOLOGICAL CORRESPONDENCE: *Determination*

ASSOCIATED CRYSTALS BY COLOR: *Howlite, serpentine*

KEYWORDS: *Fast progress toward success*

THE CRYSTAL

Rhyolite is found in igneous rock made up of volcanic silica-rich magma. It belongs to the same rock class as granite and is common around the globe. Rhyolite is the name of a ghost town on the western edge of a volcanic field, which includes Death Valley, in southwestern Nevada.

LEGENDARY USES

Although there are no specific legends for rhyolite, perhaps just as meaningful is the history surrounding the ghost town of Rhyolite, which in a way reflects the stone's ability to "rush quickly toward success." In fact, ironically rhyolite wasn't the reason for the "rush," but the discovery of gold among the rhyolitic lava flows. Within this area, gold-rush settlements quickly arose near the new mines, and the town of Rhyolite became the largest and most successful, albeit shortlived; eventually the mines went bust, and the town fell into ruin around 1912.

ATTRIBUTES AND POWERS

Considered a stone of resolution, rhyolite is best known for its ability to promote integrity, determination, and to balance one's life for successful outcomes. While it helps you fulfill your goals or make your dreams come true, it also aids in discovering what your true life journey is all about. Carry rhyolite when you know you may have to face difficult customers or clients or confront people who may try to put you off your course. This stone will help you not to rush into things without forethought, but still get you moving toward your goal so things don't stagnate. It enhances a shift in perception, and encourages you to move forward with your dreams.

HOW TO USE

Place in the south corner of your home or business to attract a "rush of interest" in your ideas.

RUBY

APPEARANCE/COLOR: *Red*

CURRENT AVAILABILITY: *Uncut widely available, polished gemstone expensive but available*

PHYSIOLOGICAL CORRESPONDENCE: *Blood and circulatory system*

PSYCHOLOGICAL CORRESPONDENCE: *Courage, passion, enthusiasm*

ASSOCIATED CRYSTALS BY COLOR: *Garnet, cinnabar*

KEYWORDS: *Dynamic success, abundant wealth*

THE CRYSTAL

Ruby is red corundum, an aluminum oxide mineral with chromium responsible for its rich, red color. The name ruby comes from the Latin word *rubeus*, meaning "red." It wasn't until 1800 that ruby was recognized as a separate stone from red spinels, tourmalines, and garnets. These were all previously thought to be ruby.

LEGENDARY USES

A symbol of passion, wealth, prosperity, and protection, the Mongolian Emperor Kublai Khan was said to have offered an entire city in exchange for a sizeable ruby. Symbolizing the sun, its glowing hue was thought to be an inextinguishable flame within the stone. Ancient Chinese legends claim the ruby would shine through even the thickest clothing and could never be hidden; while the ancient Greeks cast ruby into water to make it boil. To protect them from invading Mongols, 13th-century Burmese warriors inserted rubies into their navels, believing this would make them invincible. Sadly even the ruby could not save them.

ATTRIBUTES AND POWERS

Although an aphrodisiacal stone of passionate love, the ruby also promotes a clear mind, increased concentration, and motivation. Bestowing you with a sense of power, it enhances self-confidence and determination and guides you quickly toward prosperity and achievement. Rubies are success stones, in that they incite passion for a goal, ignite love for what and who one is, and intensify one's desire to win at all costs. It is said that provided you keep with you the smallest piece of ruby, wealth will never depart. The stone promotes the maxim of "following your bliss," and enables you to live with passion as your greatest guide.

HOW TO USE

Wear as jewelry or carry every day, touch or gently rub your ruby when you need an extra dose of courage.

SAPPHIRE (BLACK)

APPEARANCE/COLOR: *Black*

CURRENT AVAILABILITY: *Available from specialty stores*

PHYSIOLOGICAL CORRESPONDENCE: *Blood, circulatory system*

PSYCHOLOGICAL CORRESPONDENCE: *Confidence, courage*

ASSOCIATED CRYSTALS BY COLOR: *Onyx, obsidian*

KEYWORDS: *Attracts prosperity and successful enterprises*

THE CRYSTAL

Found mostly in Australia, black sapphire is an opaque variety of corundum. Less prized than blue or yellow sapphires, this black stone is often confused with onyx. But black sapphire is much harder in quality than onyx and, to the mineral experts, more useful for gemstone cutting purposes.

LEGENDARY USES

Black sapphire was used by ancient Greek necromancers, magicians, and witches as an oracle stone to foretell the future. Setting it on an altar, it was thought to have the power to channel the wisdom of the spirit world. The stone was also used in talismanic magic to cast spells or held by high priestesses of Apollo's temple at Delphi to empower them with oracular power. In ancient Egypt it was considered a stone of spiritual power and astuteness, attracting prosperity and protection when in the possession of pharaohs and royalty.

ATTRIBUTES AND POWERS

This beautiful black stone enables you to stay centered when all about you are in chaos. If you are overly sensitive to other people's conflicts of opinions or disputes, wearing or carrying black sapphire will give you the confidence to see what, if any, opportunity can be made out of deadlocks and difficult decisions, while still allowing others to take responsibility for problems of their own making. This stone enhances intuition, clarity, and self-mastery and is the ideal sapphire for grounding ideas and bringing things through to completion. Deflecting negativity, the stone will also attract success to you if you are focused and sure of your positive intention.

HOW TO USE

Place one piece of black sapphire beside a white candle to represent yin and yang energy respectively, and visualize your success story happening now to charge the energy to the universe and see the success manifest.

SAPPHIRE (YELLOW)

APPEARANCE/COLOR: *Yellow or golden*

CURRENT AVAILABILITY: *Available from specialty stores*

PHYSIOLOGICAL CORRESPONDENCE: *Detoxifier*

PSYCHOLOGICAL CORRESPONDENCE: *Intellectual power*

ASSOCIATED CRYSTALS BY COLOR: *Citrine, yellow jade*

KEYWORDS: *The stone to "sell your success"*

THE CRYSTAL

Found in Australia, Madagascar, Thailand, and Sri Lanka, the yellow sapphire is, like other corundum gems, an aluminum oxide. Next to the diamond, it is the second hardest gemstone. On the gemstone relative hardness scale, known as the Mohs Scale, at the top end at 10 is the diamond. Descending the scale shows which gemstone can scratch the one below it (but not above it). On this scale the sapphire is second to the diamond.

LEGENDARY USES

To the Hindus, the yellow sapphire is the legendary helper of their god Ganesh. By propitiating Ganesh, yellow sapphire attracts literal wealth. Throughout the ages, merchants in India and the Far East have worn or carried fine yellow sapphire to enhance their business success. Legends tell that, when worn, a portion of the stone must touch the body for its powers to work. In ancient Chinese culture, people were buried with yellow sapphire placed in their mouths to insure wealth in the next life. Once known as oriental topaz, the yellow sapphire was a status symbol of wisdom and leadership.

ATTRIBUTES AND POWERS

Yellow sapphire not only attracts wealth and financial abundance, but manifests your creative energy. It stimulates the intellect, helping you to formulate ideas and goals, promotes focus and concentration, and encourages exploration, new directions, and joyful expectation. The stone brings clarity, zest, optimism, and meaning to all that you do. The lighter yellow sapphires ensure that all new relationships get off to a good start. Darker yellow stones are excellent to hold or carry when you need to make a positive choice or persuade others. Often described as the "salesman's stone," the yellow sapphire will bestow you with the power to sell anything.

HOW TO USE

When focusing your mind on your desired success, hold a piece of yellow sapphire between your hands and then hold it out in offering to the universe in the palm of your writing hand. You will be rewarded.

SEPTARIAN

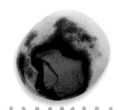

APPEARANCE/COLOR: *Mix of yellow, brown, gray*

CURRENT AVAILABILITY: *Available but expensive*

PHYSIOLOGICAL CORRESPONDENCE: *Metabolism*

PSYCHOLOGICAL CORRESPONDENCE: *Positive communication*

ASSOCIATED CRYSTALS BY COLOR: *Serpentine, brown tourmaline*

KEYWORDS: *The "speaker's stone," charismatic presence*

THE CRYSTAL

Septarian is a geode that is made up of a combination of different minerals which include calcite, aragonite, limestone, and barite. A sedimentary fossil stone, it formed as a colony of small microorganisms, similar to the polyps of coral, which give it a characteristic look of a turtle's shell. Although widely available, it occurs naturally only in Utah, Madagascar, and Morocco.

LEGENDARY USES

Also known as septaria, it takes its name from the Latin word for seven, *septem*, or *saeptum*, meaning "wall or enclosure." Millions of years ago volcanic activity disturbed the seabed and all marine life was destroyed. As the volcanic mass crashed to the seabed, mudballs formed from the various components of calcite, aragonite, limestone, and barite. As these mudballs solidified, seven fissures or wall-like cracks radiated out from the center, giving the stone, according to some, its "dragon skin" appearance. This appearance has also given rise to its legendary name of "dragon stone."

ATTRIBUTES AND POWERS

Septarian brings calming and nurturing energies and promotes feelings of joy and vitality. Used to enhance all kinds of communication, it is particularly treasured as a stone to promote brilliant public speaking. It bestows you with confidence, charisma, and an astute choice of words so that others truly listen to what you have to say too. In this way your effortless communication attracts success in whatever field you are seeking. When we change our beliefs, and change the way we communicate those beliefs, we change our world too. This stone helps you to do just that.

HOW TO USE

Wear or carry septarian whenever you are in a public place, to enhance all forms of communication and to manifest ideas and intentions.

TOURMALINE (BLACK)

APPEARANCE/COLOR: *Black, dark blueish-black*

CURRENT AVAILABILITY: *Widely available*

PHYSIOLOGICAL CORRESPONDENCE: *Brain, mental processes*

PSYCHOLOGICAL CORRESPONDENCE: *Rational thought, clear mind*

ASSOCIATED CRYSTALS BY COLOR: *Onyx, jet*

KEYWORDS: *Positive attitude toward success*

THE CRYSTAL

Black tourmaline, also known as schorl, accounts for 95 percent of all naturally occurring tourmaline. The word "schorl" was in use before the 15th century and was taken from the name of a town in Saxony, Germany, where the mineral was first found in tin mines.

LEGENDARY USES

Early medieval European magicians relied upon black tourmaline, then known as schorl, to protect them from earth demons as they cast their spells. Today this stone is still considered a talisman of protection, providing a psychic shield deflecting and dispelling negative energies, entities, or destructive forces. Used by shamans of the African, Native American, and Aboriginal peoples, black tourmaline was thought to bring healing powers to the user and provide protection from all physical danger.

ATTRIBUTES AND POWERS

With its highly protective qualities, black tourmaline enables you to maintain a positive attitude toward your goals and desires, never letting you lose your commitment to your purpose or future prospect. Wearing or carrying the stone increases physical vitality and promotes an objective view of the world and everyone in it—including yourself. It also guards against electromagnetic negativity and geopathic stress. Black tourmaline is a powerful grounding stone, promoting a sense of power and self-confidence. It will enable you to see success "written in stone" in any long-term goal, and see you through any challenging encounters.

HOW TO USE

Wear or carry black tourmaline with you in all business or relationship dealings.

CRYSTALS *for* WELL-BEING/HOME

Probably the most popular use for crystals is to manifest well-being and ensure our home and surrounding environment are in harmony. To manifest this, though, requires specific crystals which can enhance and balance our home, protect us from outside negativity, and also establish a deeper connection to the universal energy to make things happen as we want them to.

We can place a grid of crystals around the home to protect it from geopathic or other electromagnetic stresses. We can carry, wear, and use crystals to perform rituals to help heal us emotionally or bring balance to mind, body, and spirit. Whatever you consider your personal well-being to consist of, and whatever you believe creates harmony and happiness in the home, these crystals will help you to manifest exactly those intentions.

AEGIRINE

APPEARANCE/COLOR: *Greenish brown to black*

CURRENT AVAILABILITY: *Available*

PHYSIOLOGICAL CORRESPONDENCE: *Immune system*

PSYCHOLOGICAL CORRESPONDENCE: *Self-reliance*

ASSOCIATED CRYSTALS BY COLOR: *Malachite, seraphinitet*

KEYWORDS: *Protection and strength of convictions*

THE CRYSTAL

Aegirine is a sodium iron silicate, forming long prismatic or flat crystals ending in an irregular-shaped pyramid. Found principally in Malawi, Canada, Greenland, Russia, and Norway, the stone is usually opaque, but sometimes appears translucent. It is also known as acmite, from the Greek word meaning "point," due to its extremely sharp ends.

LEGENDARY USES

Discovered in Norway in the 19th century, aegirine was named after Aegir, the Norse giant of the sea, who was known to hold lavish feasts to appease the gods.

In Norse legend, wearing an aegerine amulet was thought to cure frostbite or warm the heart of those who had been betrayed or rejected in love. In Russian folklore the stone was placed beside the hearth of the home to bestow the power of the gods directly on to the family patriarch.

ATTRIBUTES AND POWERS

A stone of integrity, aegirine aligns you to your convictions and values, and gives you the confidence to follow those convictions. Black is the color of protection and invisibility. By correspondence, the stone enables you to get on with your life free from self-sabotage or malice or spite from rivals or enemies. Aegirine activates a strong, protective energy, guarding your aura and physical body. It eliminates negative thoughts and attachments, and replaces them with positive energy. Wearing the stone promotes power and strength, and relieves phobias or fears associated with human mortality. Like the giant Aegir in his feasting hall, the stone is a powerful protector against geopathic stress and/or psychic attack from others.

HOW TO USE

Hold a wand in your writing hand and point away from you, first to the north, then the east, south, and finally west. At each point say, "I manifest complete protection for myself, my home and family."

AMBER

APPEARANCE/COLOR: *Golden, yellow, brown*

CURRENT AVAILABILITY: *Common*

PHYSIOLOGICAL CORRESPONDENCE: *Throat*

PSYCHOLOGICAL CORRESPONDENCE: *Positive thinking, stability*

ASSOCIATED CRYSTALS BY COLOR: *Goldstone, golden topaz*

KEYWORDS: *Peace, balance, wholeness*

THE CRYSTAL

Transparent amber is fossilized tree resin and is usually found in irregularly shaped nodules or masses. It often contains small insects or plant specimens that were trapped millions of years ago before the resin had solidified. The amber becomes stabilized by undergoing chemical changes after it has been buried in the ground.

LEGENDARY USES

Amber has been prized since ancient Egyptian times for jewelry, talismans, amulets, and even goblets. Today, most amber is sourced from the shores of the Baltic Sea, where pine trees that exude the resin have formed the region's natural vegetation for millions of years. In Scandinavia, amber was believed to be the tears of Freyja, the Viking goddess of love and beauty. Because it is not a true stone, amber's natural warmth was deemed by some cultures to be a sign that it was a living being. In the Far East, for example, it was believed the souls of tigers metamorphosed into amber at their death and brought courage to anyone who wore the crystal.

ATTRIBUTES AND POWERS

Due to its electrostatic powers, amber is considered to be one of the most effective energy-healing crystals. It draws away toxins, pain, and disease from the body, stimulating the immune system and other natural healing mechanisms. When worn, the stone is a superb all-round crystal for well-being. Placed in the home it is also a natural purifier, absorbing negative or stagnant energy and transforming it into positive energy. Amber is also ideal for cleansing and reactivating the chakras, and is a great stone for manifesting harmony and peace at home.

HOW TO USE

Amber warms when it is touched, and generates a positive energy, so carry or wear to instill its positive glow into your life and protect you from outside stress.

AMETHYST

APPEARANCE/COLOR: *Purple, violet, lavender*

CURRENT AVAILABILITY: *Easily available*

PHYSIOLOGICAL CORRESPONDENCE: *Endocrine system*

PSYCHOLOGICAL CORRESPONDENCE: *Mental focus, decision-making, motivation*

ASSOCIATED CRYSTALS BY COLOR: *Charoite, azurite*

KEYWORDS: *All-healing, protection, imagination, insight*

THE CRYSTAL

Amethyst is a variety of quartz that forms as transparent, terminated crystals of all sizes whether as geodes, clusters, or single terminations. It is the presence of manganese in the clear quartz that produces amethyst's well-known color.

LEGENDARY USES

Ancient Greeks and Romans routinely studded their goblets with this beautiful purple crystal, believing the wine drunk from the cup would then be powerless to intoxicate them. Throughout history, amethyst has been highly esteemed for its stunning beauty and legendary powers to stimulate and soothe the mind and emotions. In the Egyptian *Book of the Dead*, it was carved into heart-shaped amulets for burial with the dead. In many Eastern cultures, it was used in temple offerings for worship, or to align with planetary and astrological influences.

ATTRIBUTES AND POWERS

The true stone of spiritual healing and enlightenment, amethyst is often used by mystics, psychics, healers, and religious leaders for its intuitive, transcendent, and spiritually restoring properties and its ability to awaken the crown and spirit chakras. Amethyst helps to stir your imagination and intuitive powers, refining thought and stimulating new ideas. It is an excellent stone for merging spiritual understanding with practical common sense. Reputed to remove evil thoughts and increase intelligence, it also enhances your creativity and passion for life. Its calming influence on the mind promotes peace, love, courage, and spiritual happiness.

HOW TO USE

Wear or carry the crystal to promote spiritual insight, invoke the magic of the universe to help make dreams come true, and to protect against thieves.

BLOODSTONE

APPEARANCE/COLOR: *Red-green*

CURRENT AVAILABILITY: *Widely available*

PHYSIOLOGICAL CORRESPONDENCE: *Lymph glands*

PSYCHOLOGICAL CORRESPONDENCE: *Flexibility, self-reliance*

ASSOCIATED CRYSTALS BY COLOR: *Green chalcedony, spider jasper*

KEYWORDS: *Living in the here and now, vitality*

THE CRYSTAL

Although sometimes referred to as heliotrope, bloodstone is defined as a dark green chalcedony with blood-like spots of red jasper or iron oxide inclusions. Heliotrope is translucent, whereas bloodstone is generally opaque with a waxy, resinous luster. It is mainly found in Armenia, India, Brazil, and the USA.

LEGENDARY USES

Known in antiquity as heliotrope, from the Greek words *helios*, meaning "sun," and *trepein*, "to attract," one ancient Greek legend recounts how the sun god, Helios, was tempted to leave the heavens forever and come down to earth when he fell in love with a mortal woman. Its use for healing, and its connection with purifying the blood can be traced back five thousand years to Mesopotamian legends. Dipped in cold water and placed on the body to aid circulation, it could transfer the power of the sun to prevent injury or disease.

ATTRIBUTES AND POWERS

Bloodstone has long been a talisman of good health and long life, and was said to bring its owner respect, good fortune, riches, and fame. It was also believed to have magical properties, including the ability to control the weather by averting lightning, conjuring storms, or summoning rain. The stone promotes self-reliance, the ability to adapt to changing circumstances, and to live in the present rather dwell on the past or worry about the future. Bloodstone calms your emotions, dispels confusion, and enhances decision-making. It is a great stone to enhance self-worth, self-confidence, and self-sufficiency.

HOW TO USE

Placed near the bed it will bring peaceful sleep and pleasant dreams.

CAXOCENITE

APPEARANCE/COLOR: *Golden brown, yellowish brown*

CURRENT AVAILABILITY: *Available but expensive*

PHYSIOLOGICAL CORRESPONDENCE: *All-round healing*

PSYCHOLOGICAL CORRESPONDENCE: *Self-confidence, spiritual growth*

ASSOCIATED CRYSTALS BY COLOR: *Golden topaz, tiger's eye*

KEYWORDS: *Powerful healing aid for holistic well-being*

THE CRYSTAL

Found though out most of Brazil, central Europe, and the USA, the stone is also known as cacoxene or cacoxitite. Caxocenite is a fibrous iron aluminum phosphate mineral with a silky luster and often appears as an inclusion in varieties of quartz such as amethyst.

LEGENDARY USES

First discovered in 1825 in a Bohemian mine, there are no legendary uses to date. However, the views of recent spiritual and healing specialists suggest that when it appears as an inclusion in quartz, it tends to amplify and promote a more powerful energy that the host stone alone can provide. So, when it appears in amethyst it increases one's ability to connect to the third-eye and crown chakras, to bring deeper spiritual awareness.

ATTRIBUTES AND POWERS

Cacoxenite in shades of brown promotes stability, patience, honesty, balance, and resourcefulness. It is the perfect energy for placing in the home to enhance any space and to create a comfortable and harmonious environment for yourself, family, and friends. It is also a great stone if you want to feel in control of your life, and protected from outside influences. Associated with the northeast and southwest areas of a home or room, the stone is best placed in these corners to amplify and promote good living. If you come across cacoxenite as an inclusion in amethyst (fairly expensive but beautiful), it will boost all forms of spiritual connection to the universal energy so that you can manifest well-being in every area of your life.

HOW TO USE

Place a piece by the front door to psychically "cleanse" guests or strangers of any negativity and to instill only harmonious energy into your home.

CHAROITE

APPEARANCE/COLOR: *Purple*

CURRENT AVAILABILITY: *Rare and expensive but still available*

PHYSIOLOGICAL CORRESPONDENCE: *Nervous system*

PSYCHOLOGICAL CORRESPONDENCE: *Acceptance, self-value*

ASSOCIATED CRYSTALS BY COLOR: *Sugilite, lepidolite*

KEYWORDS: *Spontaneity, fresh perspective*

THE CRYSTAL

A complex fibrous, silicate mineral, with swirls of lavender or violet colors and a pearly luster, its name is derived from the Chara river region in Russia, the only site in the world where it is found. Scientists are still at a loss to know why this is the only location where this rare mineral can be found.

LEGENDARY USES

As it has only recently been discovered, there are no known legends, although it is believed that since ancient times the indigenous peoples of Siberia have brewed a special tea made from the powdered stone to ward off evil spirits. The Chara river region has now become famous as the location of the charoite deposits mined from the Muran Massif of northwest Aldan in the Sakha Republic or Russia. The purple mineral was originally discovered in the 1940s during the construction of a rail tunnel, but the stone was relatively unknown to mineralogists and the gemstone world until 1978.

ATTRIBUTES AND POWERS

Charoite is often considered to be a "stone of transformation," turning negative emotions such as anger and fear into positive feelings. Charoite improves analytical abilities and the capacity for keen observation. It assists in decision-making and facilitates faster responses. Its cleansing energy aligns the heart and intellect and allows you to see yourself and others with unconditional love and acceptance. It encourages flexibility and letting go of negative vibrations, and inspires you to move forward in relationships and the way you view the world. Charoite is also beneficial in putting things into perspective and overcoming resistance to change. Wearing the stone helps you to see good possibilities in all situations.

HOW TO USE

Wear as jewelry and touch the stone daily to balance heart and crown chakras.

CHIASTOLITE (ANDALUSITE)

APPEARANCE/COLOR: *Dark brown, dark gray, red ocher*

CURRENT AVAILABILITY: *Common*

PHYSIOLOGICAL CORRESPONDENCE: *Immune system*

PSYCHOLOGICAL CORRESPONDENCE: *Security, self-awareness*

ASSOCIATED CRYSTALS BY COLOR: *Smoky quartz, idocrase*

KEYWORDS: *Grounding, reality check, stress release*

THE CRYSTAL

Chiastolite is an unusual dark brown stone with a black cross pattern occurring naturally in its structure caused by inclusions of graphite. It is a variety of andalusite, formed from aluminum ciliate in metamorphic rock. Andalusite was first found in Spain, hence its name, but both stones can be found also in Russia, the USA, Brazil, and Canada.

LEGENDARY USES

Chiastolite probably derives from the Greek word *chiastos*, meaning "cross marked" or "cruciform." Sometimes commonly called the "cross stone," early Christian believers were convinced that finding this stone was a sign that God was on your side. The stone andalusite displays the same structure and coloration, but does not have a cross within it. Also known as the "fairy stone" in medieval lore, chiastolite was considered a good luck charm to protect children from evil spirits. One legend tells that the cross was created by the tears of fairies who were unable to control their crying when they heard of the crucifixion of Jesus.

ATTRIBUTES AND POWERS

This is one of those stones that has many names, and one currently used by New Age healers is the "seeing stone." Chiastolite brings self-awareness and a non-judgmental attitude to one's own character. Wearing or carrying the stone also helps you to see the truth in other people, situations, and experiences and it also guides you to know what is the right path to follow. Chiastolite helps you see through to the end long-term projects by keeping you completely focused on the task in hand. As a stone of well-being, the stone helps you to become aware that life is in constant flux, and that all of us need to adapt to the changes that occur.

HOW TO USE

To keep a rational, grounded sense of yourself, wear this stone as a pendant. Rub it occasionally to invoke harmonious energy all around you, too.

HEMATITE

APPEARANCE/COLOR: *Silver-gray, black, brown, blue, red*

CURRENT AVAILABILITY: *Common*

PHYSIOLOGICAL CORRESPONDENCE: *Circulation*

PSYCHOLOGICAL CORRESPONDENCE: *Focus, will, strength*

ASSOCIATED CRYSTALS BY COLOR: *Apatite, smoky quartz*

KEYWORDS: *Self-esteem, magnetism, empowerment*

THE CRYSTAL

Hematite occurs in various colors: black, silver-gray, brown, reddish-brown, or red. It is the main mineral component of iron and varieties include martinet, iron rose and specularite (specular hematite). Found worldwide, and in abundance in the USA and Morocco, the best specimens are found in Cumbria in northwest England, the island of Elba, Italy, and Grischin, Switzerland. Rare prismatic forms occur in Hotazel, South Africa.

LEGENDARY USES

Hematite originates from the Ancient Greek for "blood-red stone," in reference to the rusty red of its iron ore content. However, when polished, it becomes silvery gray to black, and acts as a magnet. The pigment red ocher is a variety of hematite and has been used extensively by all civilizations for example in ancient cave art, Greek frescos, Indian mandalas, Roman drawings, Native American medicine pouches, and other spiritual symbols. The Roman historian Pliny recounted how hematite in elixir form was, for the Mesopotamians, a cure for eye disorders and liver disease.

ATTRIBUTES AND POWERS

Placed in the home or workplace, hematite is grounding and calming, and it encourages decluttering and efficient organization. It promotes original or logical thinking as well as mental focus and persistence. Emotionally, hematite decreases negativity. By balancing the chakras and bringing harmony to the holistic self it also boosts self-esteem and self-confidence. The stone enables you to come to terms with life and adopt an outlook that sees a glass half full rather than half empty.

HOW TO USE

Use a grid of hematite at each of the cardinal compass points around a property or home to invite in beneficial energy and protect you and your family from geopathic stress.

HIDDENITE

APPEARANCE/COLOR: *Green, yellow-green*

CURRENT AVAILABILITY: *Widely available*

PHYSIOLOGICAL CORRESPONDENCE: *Circulation*

PSYCHOLOGICAL CORRESPONDENCE: *Self-awareness, growth*

ASSOCIATED CRYSTALS BY COLOR: *Green obsidian, yellow muscovite*

KEYWORDS: *Compassion, communication, protection*

THE CRYSTAL

Found in Brazil, Myanmar, the USA, and Afghanistan, hiddenite is a variety of spodumene, a silicate, and is named for William Earl Hidden, who first described it in 1879 in North Carolina. Hiddenite, also referred to as green kunzite or lithia emerald, has a glasslike transparency and forms in prismatic crystals.

LEGENDARY USES

Although there are few legends due to its recent discovery, the power of this stone is, like emerald associated with its vivid green color. Green has always been a symbol of growth, fertility, prosperity, and abundance. In Chinese Feng Shui, green is associated with the element wood and the east and southeast areas of homes or rooms. The east corresponds to family, health, and well-being, while the southeast is concerned with wealth and abundance. By placing hiddenite in these areas, you will promote the essence of growth in all areas of your life.

ATTRIBUTES AND POWERS

The stone enhances new beginnings and enables you to focus on the present, letting go of the past and not worrying about the future. As a protective stone, hiddenite removes negativity, and dissolves unwanted energies and any distress or negative mental influences. Helping to reconnect loving thoughts and communication, it also recreates heartfelt love in relationships. It can even rekindle a fading romance and bring renewed ardor to a dull relationship. Hiddenite encourages someone to love with a whole heart, allowing them to see that love has no conditions and what you give out to another person is what you will receive back in kind.

HOW TO USE

Place in your home to banish geopathic stress; or wear as a pendant or carry in your pocket to bring you harmonious energy wherever you go.

JASPER, GREEN

APPEARANCE/COLOR: *Various shades of green*

CURRENT AVAILABILITY: *Widely available*

PHYSIOLOGICAL CORRESPONDENCE: *Digestive system*

PSYCHOLOGICAL CORRESPONDENCE: *Dissolves obsession*

ASSOCIATED CRYSTALS BY COLOR: *Peridot, chrysoprase*

KEYWORDS: *Harmony, inner and outer peace*

THE CRYSTAL

Found worldwide, jasper refers to an opaque microcrystalline quartz, and comes in many color variations. Green jasper has been found in archeological sites of the mid-Neolithic period dating back to 3000 BCE. It is sometimes found in fissures in igneous rock, but mostly shows as veins or cracks in volcanic outcrops.

LEGENDARY USES

Known since antiquity as "rain bringer," green jasper has long been a sought-after stone, valued for its ability to protect, strengthen, and fertilize the Earth. The first-century Roman physician Galen wore a special jasper ring to reveal his healing power. The stone was carved in the shape of a man carrying a bundle of medicinal plants. He also declared that wearing a green jasper pendant would protect the lungs and stomach, as did the Egyptian king, Nechepsus, who wore a jasper encrusted belt around his belly.

ATTRIBUTES AND POWERS

These are stones of courage, wisdom, creativity, and harmony, dissolving fear, negativity, and obsessive thinking. Wearing green jasper helps to keep yourself in balance and instill harmony among those around you. Enabling you to recognize irrational fears as simply that, the stone promotes courage and honesty, and the ability to express and accept your faults, in order to move forward. It also brings acceptance of others' faults too and a non-judgmental attitude to life. Green jasper encourages self-control and responsibility for your life path, restoring harmony in all you do.

HOW TO USE

Either wear daily, or lay a grid around your home in each of the four compass points to balance and stabilize your environment.

JET

APPEARANCE/COLOR: *Black*

CURRENT AVAILABILITY: *Common*

PHYSIOLOGICAL CORRESPONDENCE: *Lymph system*

PSYCHOLOGICAL CORRESPONDENCE: *Stability, protection from self-doubt*

ASSOCIATED CRYSTALS BY COLOR: *Onyx, black obsidian*

KEYWORDS: *Balancing, home protector, removes negativity*

THE CRYSTAL

Like amber, jet is not a true crystal, but is fossilized wood formed millions of years ago when trees were buried in sediment. Later geological erosion of the sedimentary layers revealed jet, also known as lignite, within rock and coal seams. It is found mostly in India, Europe, Russia, and the USA.

LEGENDARY USES

Ornate pieces of carved jet have been found dating as far back as 1200 BCE in prehistoric burial mounds. The ancient Greeks believed that wearing jet would insure favor from the gods, while later medieval healers believed that burning jet around a patient would cure most illnesses. The allusion to bestowing the wearer with godly favor was assimilated into Christian superstition and in the Renaissance, jet was the popular component used to create rosary beads for monks. Native American peoples, such as the Pueblo Indians, buried their dead with pieces of jet, believing it would protect their souls in the afterlife.

ATTRIBUTES AND POWERS

Throughout history jet has been considered to be a stone of protection and was used to dispel fear, evil, and violence. Its powerful protection energies are said to shield us from evil influences and geopathic stress, as well as psychic negativity from other people. Jet is considered one of the most powerful absorbers of "negative energy," reviving spirits and replacing worry with joyous thoughts. The stone also helps you to be mentally alert and to quickly find solutions to problems. Wearing or carrying polished jet enables you to take control of your life, and also attract all-round balance to the heart and home.

HOW TO USE

Place in the east corner of your home or business to help you manifest well-being in your professional and personal life.

LAZULITE

APPEARANCE/COLOR: *Dark indigo blue to sky blue*

CURRENT AVAILABILITY: *Rare, can be found in specialty stores*

PHYSIOLOGICAL CORRESPONDENCE: *Nervous system*

PSYCHOLOGICAL CORRESPONDENCE: *Self-esteem*

ASSOCIATED CRYSTALS BY COLOR: *Lazurite, sodalite*

KEYWORDS: *Focus, self-confidence, and emotional balance*

THE CRYSTAL

A blue, phosphate mineral containing magnesium, iron, and aluminum phosphate, its name derives from the Persian word *lazhward*, meaning "heavenly blue." Not to be confused with lazurite, crystals of lazulite are small and usually embedded in a matrix of other rock. The finest specimens are found in the US state of Georgia, Austria, Italy, and the Yukon Territory, Canada.

LEGENDARY USES

Although there are no obvious legends concerning lazulite, it is still often confused with lazurite and lapis lazuli. With its deeper shades of ultramarine blue it is, like other blue stones, a symbol of the power of the night sky.

ATTRIBUTES AND POWERS

Lazulite is a stone that works on many levels. It begins by gently promoting a sense of spiritual well-being and inner harmony. It then enhances emotional balance and physical health, and connects all three to bring you a sense of self-confidence and empowerment. By boosting self-esteem and intuitive powers, lazulite assists in finding solutions to problems and is a useful ally in any form of negotiation. Because it enhances your focus and self-discipline, wearing the stone reduces stress and aligns you with what is needed in the moment, rather than being preoccupied with the past or the future.

HOW TO USE

Carry or wear lazulite to promote positive thinking and harmonious relationships.

MOONSTONE

APPEARANCE/COLOR: *Clear, white, blueish-white*

CURRENT AVAILABILITY: *Widely available*

PHYSIOLOGICAL CORRESPONDENCE: *Reproductive system, pineal gland, skin, liver*

PSYCHOLOGICAL CORRESPONDENCE: *Emotional intelligence, empathy*

ASSOCIATED CRYSTALS BY COLOR: *Opal, clear spinel*

KEYWORDS: *Intuition, calmness, psychic ability*

THE CRYSTAL

Moonstone earned its name from its appearance. The stone has a kind of opalescent sheen, caused by light diffraction, that makes it seem to glow—like the full moon. This visual effect comes from its particular microstructure, a succession of fine layers of the rock feldspar.

LEGENDARY USES

Moonstones have always been thought to be linked to the power of the lunar cycle itself and so attuned to the rhythms of the oceans, too. The Romans believed that stone revealed an image of their moon goddess, Diana, and that wearing moonstone bestowed the owner with love, wisdom, prophecy, and second sight. This lovely translucent crystal has long been an amulet of protection for travelers and a gift between lovers to enhance passion.

ATTRIBUTES AND POWERS

The moon itself is a potent symbol of all things intuitive and feminine, the rhythms of nature, the sensitive, nurturing powers of all aspects of life. Moonstones bring inspiration, flashes of insight, and make you trust your intuition, so that you "see" from your "third eye" or sixth sense, rather than "react" from only your thoughts. Wearing this stone promotes clarity of mind and inner vision, and keeps you focused and balanced. White moonstone stimulates psychic perception, vision, and dream work. Generally, it is a stone that opens the mind to inspiration and attracts both spiritual and emotional harmony.

HOW TO USE

Carrying or wearing moonstone calms your emotions and encourages you to trust in the natural rhythms of life.

NUUMMITE

APPEARANCE/COLOR: *Black*

CURRENT AVAILABILITY: *Rare, available from specialty stores*

PHYSIOLOGICAL CORRESPONDENCE: *Pancreas*

PSYCHOLOGICAL CORRESPONDENCE: *Self-empowerment*

ASSOCIATED CRYSTALS BY COLOR: *Jet, onyx*

KEYWORDS: *Magical well-being, connection to the magic within you*

THE CRYSTAL

This rare black stone was first collected in Greenland in 1810 by mineralogist K. L. Giesecke. Rediscovered in the 1980s, its name means "from Nuuk," in reference to the Nuuk region of Greenland, the only place where it occurs. Formed more than three billion years ago, it is thought to be the oldest-known rock on Earth and is prized for its iridescent play of color due to the tiny flecks of minerals within.

LEGENDARY USES

Although little legendary information is available, because it is probably the oldest stone on Earth, it resonates with the earliest creation myths from ancient India and Mesopotamia when the Cosmos manifested from the Void. Used in magic spells and enchantments nuummite can similarly help you to manifest your invisible desires into reality. This is a stone for magical well-being and restoring balance holistically, as well as understanding the right use of power.

ATTRIBUTES AND POWERS

Unlocking the key to your own inner magic, nuummite is considered to be the stone to teach you true spiritual well-being. Known as the "sorcerer's stone" and worn as a talisman, it not only increases your own personal charisma, but enhances your clairvoyant or intuitive powers. Place a piece of nuummite beside you when working with divination tools to boost your ability to read the symbols and signs around you. The stone also deepens your connection to the natural world and the cosmos, relieving fear of the unknown and strengthening your contact with the spiritual realm. Offering spiritual protection, it enhances all forms of magical exploration and a feeling that you can create your own destiny and manifest your deepest desires.

HOW TO USE

To encourage a magical life, place a piece of nuummite between two white lit candles in front of a mirror. Gaze at yourself in the reflection and say: "Thank you stone for what will be, my power restored, and safe for me."

ONYX (BLACK)

APPEARANCE/COLOR: *Black*

CURRENT AVAILABILITY: *Common*

PHYSIOLOGICAL CORRESPONDENCE: *Bones*

PSYCHOLOGICAL CORRESPONDENCE: *Self-reliance, control*

ASSOCIATED CRYSTALS BY COLOR: *Jet, black obsidian*

KEYWORDS: *Holistic balance, protection in the home*

THE CRYSTAL

Although onyx is a variety of chalcedony (see page 115), its banded, marble-like appearance more closely resembles an agate. Other onyx colors, such as red, or yellow, are far more strikingly marked, whereas black onyx usually has either indistinct bands of gray or wider bands of white.

LEGENDARY USES

Onyx was popular with the ancient Greeks and Romans and it was carved into jewelry and other decorative ornaments. The name is said to derive from the Greek word meaning "fingernail" or "claw," due to the fact that the pink-banded variety of onyx resembled fingernails. In one legend, Cupid uses an arrowhead to cut the fingernails from the goddess Venus while she sleeps, leaving the clippings scattered in the sand. The Fates turned them into onyx stones so that although they were no longer immortal, they would never be destroyed.

ATTRIBUTES AND POWERS

A grounding and centering stone, onyx promotes stillness, balance, and strength and can help you concentrate while dissolving any restlessness. This is a powerful strengthening stone to help you with any learning process, and wearing black onyx instills greater self-confidence and determination. The stone brings balance to the body, harmony to the mind, and enhances intuition and instinctive power. Wearing the stone can help to reduce stress and alleviate fears and also stimulate the power of wise decision-making.

HOW TO USE

Place in the northwest corner of the home or office to bring you peace, tranquility, and beneficial visitors.

OBSIDIAN

APPEARANCE/COLOR: *Black, brown, green, blue*

CURRENT AVAILABILITY: *Readily available*

PHYSIOLOGICAL CORRESPONDENCE: *Joints, digestive system*

PSYCHOLOGICAL CORRESPONDENCE: *Truth, power issues*

ASSOCIATED CRYSTALS BY COLOR: *Black tourmaline, onyx*

KEYWORDS: *Absorbs negativity, establishes a sense of self*

THE CRYSTAL

Obsidian is formed from volcanic lava, which cooled too quickly for significant crystallization to occur. Varieties of obsidian, such as black, mahogany, apache tears, and rainbow obsidian, can all be used to equal effect, depending on the intensity of manifestation desired.

LEGENDARY USES

The Greek writer Theophrastus told how ancient Greek magicians polished obsidian to make scrying mirrors—a way of seeing into the future. A Native American Apache legend tells of a group of Apache warriors who met their deaths falling from a high cliff during a 19th-century campaign against the military. When the tears of the mourning women fell to the ground, the Great Spirits were so saddened they turned their tears to stone. Ever after these stones were known as Apache tears. It is believed that whoever carries obsidian will never cry again, as too many tears have already been shed.

ATTRIBUTES AND POWERS

All forms of obsidian can be carried to absorb negative energies and instil harmony and self-confidence. For self-empowerment, black obsidian protects you, yet reveals deeper truths. As a protective stone, it provides personal direction and acceptance of what you truly need on your life journey. Apache tears and mahogony obsidian are gentler than the black variety, and these are recommended if you fear facing suppressed emotional issues. Black obsidian, particularly, brings perseverance and determination and promotes a genuine desire to work toward agreement with others.

HOW TO USE

Place on your desk or by the front door to absorb negative energy and transmit positive power and renewed vitality.

PIETERSITE

APPEARANCE/COLOR: *Mottled browns, blue-gray*

CURRENT AVAILABILITY: *Rare but available from specialty stores*

PHYSIOLOGICAL CORRESPONDENCE: *Pinal and pituitary gland*

PSYCHOLOGICAL CORRESPONDENCE: *Truth*

ASSOCIATED CRYSTALS BY COLOR: *Idocrase, apatite*

KEYWORDS: *Trusting instincts or one's inner self*

THE CRYSTAL

Due to its swirling inclusions of golden crocidolite (which also gives tiger's eye its "chatoyancy" effect), pietersite's main body colour can range from deep brown—usually found in stones from Henan Province, China—to blue-gray when originating from Namibia, where it was first described in 1962 by mineral dealer Sid Pieters.

LEGENDARY USES

Since pietersite is a relatively recent discovery, little legendary history surrounds the stone. It is also known as the "tempest stone," perhaps, some healers say, because of its at-times stormy appearance, and the fact that it is also thought to possess a highly charged vibrational energy that aligns to stormy weather. The stone is said to protect you from bad weather if carried when driving or traveling, and to protect home and property from storms if left in a grid at each point of the compass around the home.

ATTRIBUTES AND POWERS

Apart from pietersite's protective power against bad weather, holding, wearing, or carrying the stone enhances focus and personal will. It is also a stone of vision, enabling you to "see" long term what you truly intend to manifest, and how this can aid your well-being. Promoting an instinctive or inner sense of what's right for you, pietersite dissolves others' expectations or opinions so you can see the truth of who you are. Acting as a shield against the adverse effects of technology, it is a superb proactive stone against geopathic stress, electromagnetic energy from phones, computers, electricity cables, underground trains, cellphone masts, and similar.

HOW TO USE

Carry or wear pietersite for a strong sense of personal power, or place around the home as described above as a protective shield.

PREHNITE

APPEARANCE/COLOR: *Apple green, yellow-green*

CURRENT AVAILABILITY: *Available from specialty stores*

PHYSIOLOGICAL CORRESPONDENCE: *Pancreas and insulin regulation*

PSYCHOLOGICAL CORRESPONDENCE: *Letting go, astute awareness*

ASSOCIATED CRYSTALS BY COLOR: *Jade, serpentine*

KEYWORDS: *Protective grid stone, harmony in the environment*

THE CRYSTAL

Composed of aluminum, calcium, and silicon, prehnite is brittle with an uneven surface and a vitreous to pearly luster. It is found in the veins of volcanic rock rich in magnesium and iron. The most important sources around the world are Namibia, South Africa, Australia, China, Scotland, and France.

LEGENDARY USES

Named after Dutch colonel and mineralogist H. Von Prehn, who discovered it in Cradock, Eastern Cape Province, South Africa in 1788, early traders nicknamed the gemstone "Cape Emerald" in hopes of exploiting its green color. Prehnite was originally classified as a zeolite, due to the fact that it usually forms in the same areas and under similar conditions as zeolite. There are currently no known legends, but New Age healers and crystal experts hold that it connects you directly to divine energy, and that it can promote psychic skill and even prophetic powers.

ATTRIBUTES AND POWERS

A powerfully protective stone, prehnite stimulates the life force and vitalizes the body. Wearing or carrying the stone enhances deep self-knowledge, and encourages analytical thinking. This is a stone that opens you up to your true potentials and talents, and placing it in a grid around your home will help to manifest those potentials. As a cleansing stone, prehnite motivates you to declutter your home, and also to let go of the past and start afresh.

HOW TO USE

Place in a green glass bowl and leave on a window ledge in the south corner of your home to enhance your true potential; or place in a protective grid at each of the cardinal compass points to balance or restore order to the home.

SAPPHIRE (CLEAR)

APPEARANCE/COLOR: *White or clear*

CURRENT AVAILABILITY: *Naturally clear rare; industrialized common*

PHYSIOLOGICAL CORRESPONDENCE: *Blood*

PSYCHOLOGICAL CORRESPONDENCE: *Charisma, strength, tolerance*

ASSOCIATED CRYSTALS BY COLOR: *Diamond, clear quartz*

KEYWORDS: *Integrity, truth, fairness*

THE CRYSTAL

Sapphire is a variety of corundum, an aluminum oxide mineral. When produced industrially, clear sapphire is known as leuco-sapphire. Totally natural colorless sapphire is rare, as there is usually an irregular hint of blue or yellow within all sapphire stones. Because of its extreme hardness and appearance, leuco-sapphire is often used as a diamond substitute.

LEGENDARY USES

The name corundum is of Indian origin, derived from the Sanskrit word *korund*, and used to describe opaque massive gems. With the exception of red corundum, which is ruby, all other colors of corundum are sapphires. Babylonian magicians used clear sapphires to enhance and direct their magical powers. Medieval alchemists and astrologers associated this sapphire with the element of air, and astrologers in India believed it was a portal to the heavenly realms. The Greeks identified sapphires with Apollo, and the stone was worn by the Pythia, the high priestess at Apollo's temple at Delphi, when speaking the oracles sent to her by the god.

ATTRIBUTES AND POWERS

Sapphire endows the wearer with wisdom and spiritual strength. The stone enhances clarity of thought and opens you to the deeper powers of your imagination as well as the ability to focus with logic and objectivity. Promoting a realization of who you really are, it inspires you to live with integrity and keep true to your own beliefs when faced with difficult choices or circumstances. Wearing the stone enhances the qualities of fairness, objectivity, and freedom from unnecessary need. It also enables you to truly know your hidden talents and potential for manifesting your life purpose.

HOW TO USE

Place a grid of 12 sapphires (one to signify each month of the year) in a circle on an altar or sacred place and leave for one full year to work its magic and bring you prosperity and complete well-being.

SELENITE

APPEARANCE/COLOR: *Clear*

CURRENT AVAILABILITY: *Common*

PHYSIOLOGICAL CORRESPONDENCE: *Spinal column*

PSYCHOLOGICAL CORRESPONDENCE: *Clarity, understanding*

ASSOCIATED CRYSTALS BY COLOR: *Clear quartz, clear topaz*

KEYWORDS: *Peaceful atmosphere, peaceful mind*

THE CRYSTAL

Calcium sulfate, better known as gypsum, a non-metallic mineral used to make plaster, is also found as large, clear, glass-like crystals known as selenite. Forming in sedimentary rock where seawater or underground water has evaporated, the stone is very soft and easily scratched.

LEGENDARY USES

Selenite originates from an ancient Greek word meaning "stone of the moon." The Greek moon goddess Selene fell in love with the mortal Endymion, but could only make love to him while he slept. So she left a "moon-stone" beside him so that when he woke he would remember her. Ancient astrologers and seers believed that that the power of certain transparent crystals, such as selenite and clear quartz, waxed and waned with the lunar cycle. In ancient Rome it was believed that if you kept a piece of selenite in a charm pouch it would insure fidelity "until the seas run dry." Another source describes how a tree's fruit will flourish if a stone is hung in its branches.

ATTRIBUTES AND POWERS

Translucent selenite brings clarity of mind, opening the crown and higher chakras while accessing higher guidance. It stills the mind, enables you to find peace within and also peace without. It is perfect for forming a harmony-invoking grid around the home. Place one piece at each of the compass points around your home, north, south, east, and west, and similarly, create a grid on your altar with the same layout to amplify its protective and calming power. Alternatively, place a large piece in a window ledge or by the front door to enhance peace and tranquility among family members.

HOW TO USE

Selenite dissolves in water, so never attempt to cleanse it. Leave it on a window ledge for one lunar cycle to bring love, harmony, well-being, and clarity to all relationships.

SERPENTINE

APPEARANCE/COLOR: *Green, red, brown-red, black-green*

CURRENT AVAILABILITY: *Widely available*

PHYSIOLOGICAL CORRESPONDENCE: *Pancreas and insulin regulation*

PSYCHOLOGICAL CORRESPONDENCE: *Self-control, decision-making*

ASSOCIATED CRYSTALS BY COLOR: *Bloodstone, brown aragonite*

KEYWORDS: *All-round well-being, self-reliance*

THE CRYSTAL

Serpentine stones are opaque to translucent and can have a mottled appearance resembling a snake's skin. The name refers to a group of predominantly green minerals that occur in masses of small, intergrown crystals, with two basic structures: antigorite (leafy serpentine) and chrysotile (fibrous serpentine).

LEGENDARY USES

Serpentine was used in ancient Greece and Rome as a talisman to protect against snake or scorpion bites, poison, curses, and evil. To protect high-ranking nobles or royalty against poisoners, drinking vessels were made of serpentine because it was believed that the goblet or cup would shatter to pieces if it came into contact with poison. The ancient Meso-American peoples believed that wearing serpentine would bring warriors unrivaled energy, as well as act as a protector of the soul against invisible powers.

ATTRIBUTES AND POWERS

Serpentine enables you to take control of your life rather than feel at the mercy of fate. It promotes self-empowerment and confidence in making decisions and allows you to make a choice without fear of the consequences. Like the cunning of a snake, the stone bestows you with mental wit and guile, and psychologically brings you a sense of inner harmony and outer peace. As a protective stone, serpentine is an all-round stone for harmony and self-reliance, and is said to increase the longevity of the wearer.

HOW TO USE

Placed in the garden or as a grid around the home, it promotes fertility, thriving family life, and mutual cooperation.

SODALITE

APPEARANCE/COLOR: *Blue, mottled blue, and white*

CURRENT AVAILABILITY: *Widely available*

PHYSIOLOGICAL CORRESPONDENCE: *Larynx, lymph glands*

PSYCHOLOGICAL CORRESPONDENCE: *Self-esteem, self-acceptance*

ASSOCIATED CRYSTALS BY COLOR: *Tanzanite, chrysocolla*

KEYWORDS: *Peace, calm, harmonious home*

THE CRYSTAL

Sodalite gets its name from the sodium content found within this mineral. Although occurring in many shades of blue, it is often mistaken for lapis lazuli. Sodalite rarely contains the pyrite or gold-colored specks that give lapis its sparkle.

LEGENDARY USES

This rich blue mineral was first found in Greenland in 1806. It only gained recognition as an ornamental stone after large deposits of sodalite were discovered in Ontario in the 1890s and, coinciding with a visit to Canada by Princess Margaret of England, it became nicknamed "Princess Blue," when the princess chose the stone for the interior decoration of her new home, Marlborough House. Sodalite has been known as the stone of creativity, and artists have used it in frescos.

ATTRIBUTES AND POWERS

By dissolving mental confusion, the stone enables you to think objectively about your future, and enhance emotional honesty. Amplifying intelligence and learning, sodalite also promotes inner peace and a calm temperament. Placing a piece in every room of the home enables its peace-enhancing properties to permanently flow around the environment. Keep a stone near computers and microwave ovens to reduce electromagnetic smog. Renowned for being a brilliant "psychic sponge," sodalite removes any negative energy left by past inhabitants, simultaneously promoting trust and acceptance between family members.

HOW TO USE

Carry or wear sodalite to create a harmonious atmosphere around you.

SULFUR

APPEARANCE/COLOR: *Yellow*

CURRENT AVAILABILITY: *Available from specialty stores*

PHYSIOLOGICAL CORRESPONDENCE: *Skin*

PSYCHOLOGICAL CORRESPONDENCE: *Instills self-reliance*

ASSOCIATED CRYSTALS BY COLOR: *Citrine, septarian*

KEYWORDS: *Vitality, creativity, motivation*

THE CRYSTAL

Bright yellow sulfur was once known as brimstone and is found near hot springs and volcanic regions throughout the world. For metaphysical use, choose polished and cut crystals as sulfur dust is toxic.

LEGENDARY USES

Sulfur, also written as sulphur, is referred to in the *Torah*, the central reference work of the Jewish religious tradition. English translations referred to burning sulfur as brimstone. This inspired the "fire-and-brimstone" sermons, in which priests reminded their flock of their fate of eternal damnation if they did not repent their sins. In the Old Testament, Hell was thought to smell of sulfur, perhaps due to its association with volcanic activity. The Roman historian Pliny the Elder noted that sulfur was used for fumigation and bleaching fabric, and the best-known source in the ancient world was the Greek island of Melos.

ATTRIBUTES AND POWERS

In the crystal healing world, sulfur is a stone of vitality and energy. Promoting protection and purifying the mind, it removes negative thoughts, banishes stubborn or willful attitudes, and instills a new perception and acceptance of other people's attitudes. Grounding and stabilizing, it promotes general well-being and its bright yellow color brings a vitality and *joie de vivre* to your everyday life. Placed in the south area of your home, it absorbs negativity of any kind and enables you to get motivated and creative with your goals.

HOW TO USE

Place on a top shelf or high ledge where the stone cannot be touched (it can be toxic) but can work its "fire-and-brimstone" magic in your home.

TOURMALINE, BLUE

APPEARANCE/COLOR: *Blue*

CURRENT AVAILABILITY: *Available from specialty stores*

PHYSIOLOGICAL CORRESPONDENCE: *Skin, immune system*

PSYCHOLOGICAL CORRESPONDENCE: *Positive attitude*

ASSOCIATED CRYSTALS BY COLOR: *Blue sapphire, lapis lazuli*

KEYWORDS: *Sense of purpose, luck and empowerment*

THE CRYSTAL

In common with all tourmalines, coveted blue tourmaline has a trigonal crystal structure. It is much rarer than the other tourmalines in this, the most colorful of all gemstone groups, and forms in shades of light to dark blue. Brazil is the major source of most blue tourmaline, including the much-prized turquoise variety known as the Paraiba stone.

LEGENDARY USES

In ancient indigenous cultures including tribal peoples of Africa and Australia, tourmaline was thought to bring healing power to the user and provide protection from all dangers. Its popularity as a gemstone began in 1876, when mineralogist and collector George F. Kunz sold a tourmaline to Tiffany & Co. in New York, and the gem's desirability spread. More recently, with its versatile energy properties, it has become a favorite stone for crystal healers.

ATTRIBUTES AND POWERS

Blue tourmaline promotes clear and honest communication, and gives you the courage to speak from the heart. Wearing the stone encourages an open mind and tolerance for others' differences. Placing a grid of stones in your home will bring harmony to the family and balance the environment. Use the paler, turquoise-colored crystals to enhance any space that you use for relaxing. With its power to manifest a happy attitude and positive sense of self, blue tourmaline allows you to see how to let your life unfold and flow to restore well-being.

HOW TO USE

Place a circle of blue tourmaline stones at each compass point of your home to activate a balanced environment.

CRYSTALS *for* LOVE

· ·

We all want to manifest in our life that enigmatic, quality love. Some of us are lucky enough to feel blessed with a loving marriage, or a long-term commitment, yet we may feel that we are misunderstood, or not "loved" for who we truly are; we may be unable to communicate our feelings or fear hearing words we don't wish to hear from a current admirer. We may want love to become a reality, rather than a possibility, as is often the issue with long-distance relationships. If we love someone but have no physical contact, our imagination works overtime, wondering why they haven't texted us ten times a day and what they might be up to.

Using crystals helps you to manifest the truth of the relationship and to see it for what it really is. Working with these stones can also "make a relationship a physical reality" if you truly believe that you are going to be with that person. Some of us want only eternal romance and the magic of passionate affairs or the "perfect" lover. Idealists abound as do realists, but what almost all of us seek is to create a unique relationship with someone, where we are free from fears, doubts, and jealous imaginings. It's a hard love road we travel along, but the following stones can help you manifest your true desires. But before you focus your intention, first ask yourself two questions: What does love really mean for you, and what kind of love relationship do you truly seek?

AMAZONITE

APPEARANCE/COLOR: *Blue, turquoise, green with light veins*

CURRENT AVAILABILITY: *Widely available*

PHYSIOLOGICAL CORRESPONDENCE: *Nervous system*

PSYCHOLOGICAL CORRESPONDENCE: *Balanced judgment*

ASSOCIATED CRYSTALS BY COLOR: *Turquoise, blue lace agate*

KEYWORDS: *Loving communication*

THE CRYSTAL

Amazonite, also known as amazon stone, is a green to blue-green variety of microcline, a feldspar mineral. It ranges in hue from bright green to paler shades of turquoise, often with white, yellow, or gold-colored veins, and it can also be translucent or opaque.

LEGENDARY USES

In ancient India, Egypt, and Mesopotamia amazonite was used as a decorative material for buildings and was a popular amulet stone. An amazonite scarab ring was found among Pharaoh Tutankhamun's treasures, and in biblical tradition, the stone was believed to be the third stone in the breastplate of the High Priest, Aaron. One legend says it gets its name from adorning the shields of the Amazonians, a formidable tribe of Bronze Age female warriors. Some stories claim the more ferocious women had one breast removed to be more effective in their archery skills, and rubbed their wounds with a polished amazonite to avoid infection.

ATTRIBUTES AND POWERS

A stone of courage, Amazonite allows you to discover your own integrity, and to move beyond fear of judgment or confrontation with others. Promoting freedom of expression, it can help you to set strong and clear boundaries in love relationships. Wearing the stone revitalizes the heart and throat chakras and invokes loving communication on all levels. Stirring compassion for others, the stone enables you to see both sides to any dilemma, and to accept differences of opinion without taking things personally. With its power to raise self-esteem, amazonite enhances your ability to communicate your feelings more effectively.

HOW TO USE

Share unconditional communication with a lover or friend by giving them a stone, and when together, hold your stones and speak the truth.

BRONZITE

APPEARANCE/COLOR: *Earthy brown*

CURRENT AVAILABILITY: *Common*

PHYSIOLOGICAL CORRESPONDENCE: *Blood, circulatory system*

PSYCHOLOGICAL CORRESPONDENCE: *Compassion*

ASSOCIATED CRYSTALS BY COLOR: *Smoky quartz, tiger's eye*

KEYWORDS: *Non-judgmental love and acceptance*

THE CRYSTAL

Bronzite is composed of enstatite and hypersthene, a mix of magnesium and magnesium iron silicate. With its inclusions of hematite and geothetite, bronzite radiates sparkling bronze flashes named "schiller." Polishing the stone exaggerates its metallic luster.

LEGENDARY USES

Bronzite's high iron content was sacred to the ancient Vedic Indians who believed it was a gift from the gods. Similarly, in Buddhist Tibet, ritual objects were usually made of iron, because they were thought to have been tempered by the celestial gods. Many of the *vajras*—ritual weapons representing the thunderbolt and the diamond—were placed with the statue of a god, and were forged from meteorite iron, known to the ancient priests as "sky iron." The high-altitude, desolate landscape of Tibet is littered with these meteorite fragments.

ATTRIBUTES AND POWERS

Although bronzite is often used to protect against geopathic stress, it is also a great stone to attract the right kind of lover or partner. Increasing self-esteem and self-worth, wearing bronzite means you can go out into the world and attract the same goodness back to you. Known as a "stone of courtesy," bronzite promotes non-judgmental attitude toward the people you meet. It helps you to retain your own power, without trying to force your opinions on others, and helps you to see that other people may have a different perspective on life from you. When you wear this stone, you can successfully attract potential partners to you without either of you resorting to power games.

HOW TO USE

Place in the southwest corner of your home to promote self-acceptance and compassion, and wear to enhance your positive attitude wherever you go.

CHRYSOCOLLA

APPEARANCE/COLOR: *Green, turquoise, blue*

CURRENT AVAILABILITY: *Common*

PHYSIOLOGICAL CORRESPONDENCE: *Lungs*

PSYCHOLOGICAL CORRESPONDENCE: *Heals heartbreak*

ASSOCIATED CRYSTALS BY COLOR: *Turquoise, blue sapphire*

KEYWORDS: *Enhances and attracts compassion, forgiveness*

THE CRYSTAL

The name of this stone is believed to come from the Greek words *chrysos*, gold, and *kolla*, glue, referring to its use to solder gold. Often found in association with malachite and azurite, chrysocolla is a copper phyllosilicate mineral, and is found in Russia, Chile, Mexico, and Arizona.

LEGENDARY USES

In ancient Egypt, carrying the stone was thought to protect the mind and body from curses and evil thoughts, and so was worn by tradesmen and pharaohs alike in all important negotiations. As a stone of wise council and peace, the Native American shamans placed the stone at the center of a medicine wheel to help align with the forces of nature and the spirit world to insure good harvests.

ATTRIBUTES AND POWERS

If you need a stone to help you get over a break-up, or to help you forgive and be at peace with yourself and others, this is the stone for you. Not only does it "glue" back together your own broken feelings, making you feel whole again, but enhances any new emotional bonds. Chrysocolla encourages us to share our insights, and also to know the value of when to express one's feelings and when to stay silent. We can, after all, speak and say nothing, or remain silent and speak volumes. This stone's soothing energy dispels highly charged emotional situations, angry words, or bitter disputes, and enables you to manifest your feelings without fear of being made a fool.

HOW TO USE

Wear as jewelry or carry in your pocket to manifest harmonious and honest dialog in all love relationships.

GARNET

APPEARANCE/COLOR: *Deep red*

CURRENT AVAILABILITY: *Common*

PHYSIOLOGICAL CORRESPONDENCE: *Sexual organs*

PSYCHOLOGICAL CORRESPONDENCE: *Physical love*

ASSOCIATED CRYSTALS BY COLOR: *Ruby, red spinel*

KEYWORDS: *Passion, bliss, sexual excitement*

THE CRYSTAL

The word "garnet" is derived from the Latin name for the pomegranate—*granatum*—and the granular varieties of garnet resemble the seeds of that fruit. Also known as "carbuncles," meaning coal-fire, red garnets are the ultimate stone to stir love in another's heart.

LEGENDARY USES

The fiery-red carbuncle is at the heart of many ancient legends, including how it was suspended in Noah's Ark to diffuse light. The Greeks called the carbuncle the "lamp stone" and it was believed to give one the power to see in the dark if worn as a pendant. Throughout the medieval period, low libido and/or sexual disorders were thought to be relieved by the application of garnet directly to the genital organs. The 17th-century French Princess Palatine discovered her husband, the brother of King Louis XIV, applying garnets to his body in this way. He asked her not to reveal this to anyone; instead she told the whole court and wrote about it in her famous letters.

ATTRIBUTES AND POWERS

Garnet is the stone of sensuality, sexuality, and passion. With the incredible power to produce intense feelings of desire in an admirer, garnet revitalizes feelings, promotes self-esteem, and controls anger or jealousy. Several varieties of garnet have specific powers, including the most famous one, pyrope garnet, which is a mesmerizing stone, described as "living fire." As a stone of inspiration, when worn or carried, garnet bestows you with vitality, charisma, and the ability to increase your popularity and draw love to you. Almandine garnet is a talisman of protection, but also a stone of physical love, stimulating the sex drive, and inspiring love and devotion.

HOW TO USE

Wear or carry garnet every day for one lunar cycle to attract new romance into your life or to draw a lover closer to you.

GOSHENITE

APPEARANCE/COLOR: *Colorless*

CURRENT AVAILABILITY: *Common*

PHYSIOLOGICAL CORRESPONDENCE: *Mental processes*

PSYCHOLOGICAL CORRESPONDENCE: *Clarity, honesty*

ASSOCIATED CRYSTALS BY COLOR: *Selenite, clear quartz crystal*

KEYWORDS: *Fidelity in love*

THE CRYSTAL

Named after significant deposits were discovered in Goshen, Massachusetts, the stone is an aluminum beryllium silicate mineral. It forms in prismatic or vertically striated crystals, sometimes terminated by small pyramidal faces. Goshenite is transparent to translucent, with a vitreous luster.

LEGENDARY USES

Beryl crystals were favored for scrying and crystal-gazing by ancient Greek and Roman seers and magicians. The favorite shade used by ancient seers was the pale blue aquamarine, but the most transparent were better for seeing into the future, such as clear quartz (see page 99). These spheres of crystal were supposedly under the influence of the moon, and similarly the moon exerted its power when used by medieval sorcerers for love spells. When the moon waxed, goshenite had more power, thus attracting love, and when the moon waned, the power lessened and so love might be withheld.

ATTRIBUTES AND POWERS

Colorless goshenite is a feminine crystal of the moon and associated with motherhood. Wearing it enhances your ability to take a clear and honest look at what you want in a love relationship, and also enables you to see the sincerity of others. It promotes truthfulness above all, and encourages fidelity in relationships, honoring loyalty and respect, perseverance, and open-heartedness. You can also work with the stone to promote creative thinking, originality, and artistic expression. An excellent stone for stabilizing relationships, it bestows the wearer with a truly loving energy.

HOW TO USE

Place in the southwest corner of your home to promote romantic encounters and clarity in love affairs.

KUNZITE

APPEARANCE/COLOR: *Pink, light violet, lilac, yellow*

CURRENT AVAILABILITY: *Once rare, available in specialty stores*

PHYSIOLOGICAL CORRESPONDENCE: *Heart, circulation*

PSYCHOLOGICAL CORRESPONDENCE: *Self-expression*

ASSOCIATED CRYSTALS BY COLOR: *Pink tourmaline, blue lace agate*

KEYWORDS: *Unconditional love*

THE CRYSTAL

Found predominantly in Russia, Brazil, the USA, and Madagascar, the stone was named for the mineralogist George F. Kunz, who first described the stone in 1902. Kunzite is a pink to violet variety of the silicate mineral spodumene. It has a glassy transparency and forms in flattened prismatic crystals with vertical striations.

LEGENDARY USES

As kunzite is a relatively recent find, there are no available legends. But it is a truly important stone for manifesting love, with many attributes. Kunzite opens the heart to all the energies of love—love of self, of others, of humanity, plants, animals, the Earth and everything it contains. By embracing all other types of love, you can connect to the essence of the universal energy in everything. The stone's soothing color removes anger or resentment, and can aid deep reflection.

ATTRIBUTES AND POWERS

For manifesting new romance and unconditional love, the pink and lilac colors are the most powerful. To attract new love romance or any kind of new relationships, wear or carry pink kunzite. It boosts your sensuality, and can also help overcome resentment or a feeling of loss in any relationship break-up. The stone enhances your charisma and attracts romance to you, especially if unconditional love is what you seek right now. Its high vibrational energy encourages letting go of fears and sorrows that prevent you from moving on, and for accepting the here and now. Kunite enhances free expression of feelings, healing the mind and heart, and allows you to be receptive to new gifts and opportunities in love.

HOW TO USE

Place three pieces of kunzite in a triangle grid (main point to the north). Place a lighted pink candle in the middle and ask the crystals to manifest love.

KYANITE

APPEARANCE/COLOR: *Blue (also pink and gray)*

CURRENT AVAILABILITY: *Widely available*

PHYSIOLOGICAL CORRESPONDENCE: *Thyroid, adrenal glands, urogenital system*

PSYCHOLOGICAL CORRESPONDENCE: *Insight, clarity of thought, speaking the truth*

ASSOCIATED CRYSTALS BY COLOR: *Blue quartz, blue moonstone*

KEYWORDS: *Communication in love, release from illusions*

THE CRYSTAL

Kyanite derives from the Greek word *kyanos*, meaning "deep blue," and was once commonly called *disthene*, meaning "two strengths." The stone has a dual hardness depending on whether it is cut parallel to its long axis (softer) or perpendicular to it (harder). Its striated structure is formed of aluminum silicate.

LEGENDARY USES

Kyanite is often mistaken for sapphire. One apocryphal story tells of how the Sita Devi of Kapurthala, also known as Princess Karam, one of the most glamorous women of the mid-20th century, was given a necklace of apparently rare sapphires to add to her growing treasury of jewels. One day she dropped the necklace down a marble staircase and many of the stones shattered, proving they were not sapphires but highly brittle kyanite stones which had been badly mounted in their cabochons.

ATTRIBUTES AND POWERS

Associated with the throat chakra, kyanite is excellent for communication on all levels. This extraordinary crystal also enhances telepathic and psychic abilities, providing a link for transmitting or receiving loving, healing energy. When you wear or carry this stone, any sense of external fate becomes mere illusion, and you begin to realize that you create your own destiny. As a love stone, kyanite enables you to make decisions without feeling you need to compromise, to see the truth of any relationship, and sometimes even glimpse its outcome. Most importantly, it promotes clear communication and a deeper or, unspoken, connection with the one you love.

HOW TO USE

Kyanite can be worn as a pendant to enhance all forms of communication with loved ones.

LAPIS LAZULI

APPEARANCE/COLOR: *Rich, deep blue with gold flecks*

CURRENT AVAILABILITY: *Widely obtained, but the more gold flecks the more expensive*

PHYSIOLOGICAL CORRESPONDENCE: *Immune system*

PSYCHOLOGICAL CORRESPONDENCE: *Self-expression, endurance*

ASSOCIATED CRYSTALS BY COLOR: *Chrysocolla, blue tourmaline*

KEYWORDS: *Bonding, accepting others and self for who you/they are*

THE CRYSTAL

The name of this stone comes from the Latin word for stone, *lapis*, and the ancient Persian word for blue, *lazhward*. It is rock formed by a combination of minerals, mostly lazurite, sodalite, and calcite, with gold flecks of pyrite. Lower-grade lapis lazuli is lighter blue with more white than gold flecks, and is sometimes called denim lapis.

LEGENDARY USES

Until the 19th century, ground lapis lazuli was the source of the painter's finest deep-blue pigment, known as ultramarine. It was very costly, and was often used by Renaissance painters to depict their subject—for example, the flowing robes of the Virgin Mary—or the sea and sky. When lapis was first introduced in Europe, it was called *ultramarinum*, meaning "beyond the sea." In ancient pre-Columbian America, the stone was a symbol of the starry night, and in ancient Persia it was used for protection against the evil eye. Similarly, medieval European magicians and astrologers believed wearing lapis lazuli, which symbolized the heavens, would protect against dark powers and attract the favor of the "daimons" of light and wisdom.

ATTRIBUTES AND POWERS

A stone of truth, lapis lazuli is worn for all forms of loving communication and to insure long-term bonds. Bringing harmonious energy to lovers, it also encourages objectivity, clarity, creative thinking, and compromise. Lapis lazuli is associated with Jupiter, amplifying wisdom and leadership qualities. It can also help to put an end to marital disputes, promoting solidarity and agreement. Lapis lazuli promotes self-awareness, and for standing up for oneself or taking charge of one's life. To manifest solid, long-lasting bonds, wear a lapis lazuli ring. Its energy instills trust and emotional harmony by dissolving self-doubts, defensive reactions, and emotional game-playing.

HOW TO USE

Place lapis lazuli under the bed to help you create a lasting bond with the one you love.

MAGNETITE

APPEARANCE/COLOR: *Black, browny-gray*

CURRENT AVAILABILITY: *Common*

PHYSIOLOGICAL CORRESPONDENCE: *Blood, circulation*

PSYCHOLOGICAL CORRESPONDENCE: *Tenacity, endurance*

ASSOCIATED CRYSTALS BY COLOR: *Tektite, brown tourmaline*

KEYWORDS: *A magnet for love*

THE CRYSTAL

Magnetite is a very common iron oxide mineral that is found in igneous, metamorphic, and sedimentary rocks. It is the most commonly mined ore of iron. This stone is common and occurs throughout the world, but most impressively in Mauritania, West Africa, where magnetite forms an entire mountain with a magnetic field so powerful that no compass works.

LEGENDARY USES

Some say the word magnet derives from the Greek *Magnes lithos*, meaning "Magnesian stone," as it can be found in the Magnesia region in Thessaly. It is also known as lodestone, meaning "the stone that leads the way," referring to the fact that magnetite can be naturally magnetized and so gave the ancients an early form of magnetic compass. Another legend, according to the Roman writer Pliny, who cites Nicander, is that the word magnet derives from the name of a shepherd, Magnes, who discovered that the iron nails in his shoes and the ferrule on the end of his staff were "magnetized" to the ground of Mount Ida, dense with the magnetic ore.

ATTRIBUTES AND POWERS

Magnetite is a potent stone for manifestation, helping you to attract what you most desire, including desirable situations, people, or simply just loving attention. It also attracts romantic suitors, commitment, loyalty, and can promote a strong emotional connection with someone. Wearing the stone activates a deep and powerful bond with someone when you most need it. It also alleviates fear, self-doubt, and over-attachment to the past. Inspiring objectivity, magnetite cuts through illusions and gives you the power to make love choices without being swayed by your own fantasies or someone else's seductive wiles.

HOW TO USE

Wear or carry magnetite with you on a first date to attract and stimulate desire.

MORGANITE

APPEARANCE/COLOR: *Pink*

CURRENT AVAILABILITY: *Common*

PHYSIOLOGICAL CORRESPONDENCE: *Nervous system*

PSYCHOLOGICAL CORRESPONDENCE: *Emotional honesty*

ASSOCIATED CRYSTALS BY COLOR: *Pink quartz, rhodoschrosite*

KEYWORDS: *Abundant love*

THE CRYSTAL

Morganite is the pink variety of beryl. It is known for its transparent pink color, often soft pink, violet-pink, or pale salmon. In rare cases, it can display chatoyancy (resembling the band of reflected light in a cat's eye), and is often cut to highlight this effect.

LEGENDARY USES

Discovered in California in the early 1900s and, soon after, on Madagascar, the crystal was known as pink beryl until 1911 when, at the suggestion of George F. Kunz, then chief gemologist at Tiffany & Co., it was renamed morganite. This was in honor of a Tiffany patron, the financier and gem collector J. P. Morgan, for his gemological and mineral contributions to the American Museum of Natural History in New York.

ATTRIBUTES AND POWERS

Morganite promotes determination, commitment, and caring. Its soothing color calms feelings of anger or resentment. Pink is also the color of new love, new romance, and new relationships. Wearing the stone increases sensual love, and can help overcome heartache. Morganite also attracts abundant love into your life, and helps to maintain that love with positive thoughts and actions. As a crystal of manifestation, it may be used to attract one's soulmate or deepen a current relationship. It inspires joy and reverence for life and encourages one to move forward with renewed purpose and an open heart.

HOW TO USE

Place a circle of seven pieces of morganite in the southwest corner of your home to attract new love into your life or revitalize an existing one.

PEARL

APPEARANCE/COLOR: *White, pearl luster*

CURRENT AVAILABILITY: *Common*

PHYSIOLOGICAL CORRESPONDENCE: *Ovaries, womb*

PSYCHOLOGICAL CORRESPONDENCE: *Truth, fidelity*

ASSOCIATED CRYSTALS BY COLOR: *Moonstone, opal*

KEYWORDS: *Vitalizing feminine power to attract love*

THE CRYSTAL

Unlike crystals that form in the Earth, pearls grow in oysters and mussels. When a grain of sand or other irritant gets inside the shell, the mollusk secretes layer upon layer of nacre around the irritant until it gradually builds up to form a pearl. Light reflecting from these overlapping layers produces the characteristic iridescent glow.

LEGENDARY USES

In ancient Vedic texts, the primeval forces of Heaven and Earth created the pearl. Before it floated into the Void, it was fertilized by a flash of lightning and became the daughter of the moon. Legend tells that Cleopatra only drank wine that was dusted with ground pearls to protect herself from poisoning. In the Bible's Book of Job, there is a saying, "the price of wisdom is above pearls," while Lucifer is said to have broken his teeth on pearls after being unable to resist trying to eat them.

ATTRIBUTES AND POWERS

Historically a symbol of purity, innocence, and faith, pearls enhance personal integrity and bring clarity, sincerity, truth, and loyalty. Said to stimulate one's femininity and to assist in self-acceptance, wearing pearls can promote self-value and confidence, lifting your spirits and enhancing your feminine charm. Aligned to the moon's cycle, wearing pearls when the moon is waxing will help you to seduce new admirers to your side; worn during the waning moon, pearls can help you move a relationship toward a new beginning, or toward closure if that is what is truly desired.

HOW TO USE

On a full moon night, place five pearls in the shape of a five-pointed star, with the main point facing upward. Light a white candle in the middle and make your love wish. If you truly believe in manifesting this wish, it will come true.

PECTOLITE (BLUE)

APPEARANCE/COLOR: *Soft blue or green*

CURRENT AVAILABILITY: *Widely available*

PHYSIOLOGICAL CORRESPONDENCE: *Cartilage*

PSYCHOLOGICAL CORRESPONDENCE: *Serenity, acceptance*

ASSOCIATED CRYSTALS BY COLOR: *Aquamarine, moss agate*

KEYWORDS: *Synchronicity, soulmate encounters*

THE CRYSTAL

Blue pectolite is the rare, gem-quality variety of the commonly occurring silicate mineral pectolite. It forms as needle-like crystals, grown together in a solid mass, and forms in cavities within basaltic lava. Copper or manganese intrusions produce beautiful translucent shades of soft blues with whorls or streaks of white.

LEGENDARY USES

Pectolite was first described in 1828 in the Italian Alps and as such there are no legends. Particularly fine quality pectolite can be found in New Jersey. Collectible light blue pectolite comes only from the Dominican Republic, where it is sold under its trademarked name, Larimar. In 1974, the Dominican who rediscovered it after its original find in 1916, used the first letters of his daughter's name, Larissa, and the Spanish word for the sea, *mar*, to create the name Larimar. Pectolite derives from the Greek words *pektos*, meaning "compacted," and *lithos*, meaning "stone."

ATTRIBUTES AND POWERS

As a soothing Water element stone, blue pectolite calms hot tempers and instills a sense of peace and serenity in the wearer. Blue pectolite is an excellent stone for finding a soulmate. Not only does it help to heal unresolved issues or fears, but also connects you to the cycles of nature, and the feminine principle. By doing so, the stone enables you to manifest true love and weave into the synchronicity of meeting your perfect partner. If you are looking for a stone which enables you to manifest positive change in your relationships—whether letting go of someone or restarting your life with someone new, this is a great stone to wear or carry.

HOW TO USE

Place in the southwest corner of your home to attract a new lover or soulmate into your life.

QUARTZ (ROSE)

APPEARANCE/COLOR: *Rose-pink*

CURRENT AVAILABILITY: *Common*

PHYSIOLOGICAL CORRESPONDENCE: *Heart*

PSYCHOLOGICAL CORRESPONDENCE: *Emotional healing*

ASSOCIATED CRYSTALS BY COLOR: *Rhodochrosite, pink tourmaline*

KEYWORDS: *Unconditional love, new romance*

THE CRYSTAL

Rose quartz, not to be confused with pink quartz, is a silicon dioxide crystal, and one of the most common varieties of the quartz family. It is found in abundance around the world and occurs only in massive form, with no crystal faces, edges, or terminations.

LEGENDARY USES

Ancient Egyptians believed rose quartz would promote a perfect complexion, and it was ground to a fine powder to make facial masks. Also known as the "heart stone," rose quartz has long been an important stone for carving love talismans and statues in the Far East and may have been used as a love token as early as 6000 BCE. According to one legend, when Adonis, lover of the Greek goddess Aphrodite, was attacked by the jealous Ares, god of war, Aphrodite tried to save Adonis and caught her arm on a thorn bush. As their mingled blood fell to earth, it stained clear quartz the rose-pink color.

ATTRIBUTES AND POWERS

Highly effective in attracting new love, romance, and intimacy, rose quartz is well known for its power to create a closer bond between lovers. If you are looking for love, rose quartz may also be placed by the bed or in the relationship corner of the home (the southwest) to restore trust and harmony, and to encourage unconditional love. As a stone of love, tenderness, and sensuality, rose quartz is a powerful aphrodisiac, stimulating sensual imagination. It helps to prevent fear or rejection, and allows you to see that love is about giving others space and not expecting too much too soon. However, if you want to manifest a new romance, this is the stone to carry or wear on a daily basis.

HOW TO USE

Place a piece of rose quartz in the southwest corner of every room in your home, as well as on your desk to attract and manifest the right kind of love for you at any moment of time.

RHODOCHROSITE

APPEARANCE/COLOR: *Pink, rose-red, orange*

CURRENT AVAILABILITY: *Easily obtained*

PHYSIOLOGICAL CORRESPONDENCE: *Respiration*

PSYCHOLOGICAL CORRESPONDENCE: *Emotional honesty*

ASSOCIATED CRYSTALS BY COLOR: *Pink tourmaline, rhodolite*

KEYWORDS: *Soul-mate attraction*

THE CRYSTAL

Rhodochrosite is a manganese carbonate mineral of the calcite group. Its name derives from the Greek words *rhodon,* meaning "rose," and *khros,* meaning "color," referring to its vivid pink or rose-red color. It has a vitreous and pearly luster, often banded in layers ranging from white or light pink.

LEGENDARY USES

Sometimes known as Inca rose, the stone was believed to have been discovered in the pre-Colombian 13th-century silver mines in what is now northern Argentina. One of the earliest Inca rulers, Viracocha, was credited with the discovery of the rose-red stone. Believing the stone to be formed from the blood of the Incas' ancestral founders, it was sacred to the people ever after. Another legend tells of how a cave deep inside the Andes is a secret home to a rhodochrosite heart-shaped boulder. It is believed to be the heart of Mother Earth, beating once every two hundred years.

ATTRIBUTES AND POWERS

Rhodochrosite emanates one of the most tender and loving energies of any stone, soothing the heart and comforting the soul. Symbolizing selfless love, wearing, carrying, or meditating with rhodochrosite frees you from emotional stress. It allows for spontaneous expression of feelings and can enhance passion and sexuality. Rhodochrosite is a great stone for manifesting new love in one's life, whether a friend, romantic partner, or soulmate. Promoting success in your quest for emotional happiness, it can help you express love toward others without fear of rejection, allowing you to face the truth about yourself and others with loving awareness.

HOW TO USE

Wear to attract new love; place beside your bed to manifest romantic dreams.

RHODOLITE

APPEARANCE/COLOR: *Rose, raspberry red, pale violet*

CURRENT AVAILABILITY: *Widely available*

PHYSIOLOGICAL CORRESPONDENCE: *Blood circulation*

PSYCHOLOGICAL CORRESPONDENCE: *Trust, inspiration*

ASSOCIATED CRYSTALS BY COLOR: *Rhodoschrosite, rhodonite*

KEYWORDS: *Enhances sexuality, manifests desire*

THE CRYSTAL

Rhodolite is a mixture of two minerals, pyrope and almandine garnet. Its name is derived from the Greek words for "rose" and "stone." It shimmers with all the brilliance and fire of the garnets, with colors ranging from rose through raspberry to pale violet.

LEGENDARY USES

Greek mythology speaks of rose-red garnets which, through the influence of the gods Zeus and Aphrodite, heal emotional rifts between lovers. In ancient India, garnets were used in weaponry because they were believed to have powerful magical powers to kill all evil. Victorian widows wore garnets to show their undying love for their departed spouses and luxury jewelers, including Fabergé and Tiffany, began to use rhodolite in their designs.

ATTRIBUTES AND POWERS

Known as a stone of inspiration, rhodolite stimulates one's sense of self-worth and awareness of one's own talents. It encourages love, kindness, and compassion, and promotes spiritual growth. Rhodolite soothes and heals the emotions, unblocking the inability to receive love. Light red or pink rhodolite brings the energy rays of determination, commitment, and caring. Its soothing color calms feelings of anger or resentment, and can help you to meditate and reflect. Wearing the pinker shades of rhodolite promotes charisma and desirability. The darker, raspberry variety of rhodolite will enhance all forms of sexual desire and encourage seductive encounters or physical relationships to flourish.

HOW TO USE

Wear or carry rhodolite to seduce and to achieve your goal to manifest new romance.

RHODONITE

APPEARANCE/COLOR: *Red or pink*

CURRENT AVAILABILITY: *Easily available*

PHYSIOLOGICAL CORRESPONDENCE: *Bones, joints*

PSYCHOLOGICAL CORRESPONDENCE: *Self-love, confidence*

ASSOCIATED CRYSTALS BY COLOR: *Garnet, ruby*

KEYWORDS: *Passionate exchange*

THE CRYSTAL

Rhodonite commonly occurs as compact masses of rose-red stone (the name comes from the Greek *rhodon*, meaning "rosy"), streaked or layered with black or white veins showing the presence of manganese. The surface can sometimes tend toward a shade of brown because of oxidation.

LEGENDARY USES

In Russia up until the late 18th century this rose-red stone was known among the indigenous peoples of the Urals as the "eagle stone." Observing eagles carrying pieces of the stone to build and protect their eyries, it became a local superstition to place an amulet inside a baby's crib to protect the child against evil. Prized by Russian tsars for making ornamental tableware and beautiful jewelry, it became the national stone of Russia in 1913.

ATTRIBUTES AND POWERS

As a stone that nurtures love, wearing or carrying rhodonite protects against envy and jealousy; it brings purpose, cooperation, and generosity of spirit. Rhodonite is highly recognized as an emotional healer and for acceptance of one's own emotional state. It grounds, stabilizes and brings self-confidence in all love relationships. Wearing the stone alerts you to circumstances where something, or someone, is not all it seems, providing the "wake-up call" needed to do something positive about it. Carry rhodonite to stop others blaming you for their own failings, and to see that revenge and retaliation are self-destructive. Wear the stone to transform any negative energy into true sexual union and passion between two lovers.

HOW TO USE

To manifest a true passionate exchange of energy, place a grid of four rhodonite pieces, one in each corner of your bedroom, and a fifth white quartz crystal under your bed, mattress, or pillow to amplify the power.

SAPPHIRE (PINK)

APPEARANCE/COLOR: *Light pink*

CURRENT AVAILABILITY: *Available from specialty stores*

PHYSIOLOGICAL CORRESPONDENCE: *Circulatory system*

PSYCHOLOGICAL CORRESPONDENCE: *Emotional mastery*

ASSOCIATED CRYSTALS BY COLOR: *Pink tourmaline, rose quartz*

KEYWORDS: *Fast-acting love attractor*

THE CRYSTAL

Sapphire is a variety of corundum, an aluminum oxide mineral, and may be transparent or opaque. Pink corundum is now known as pink sapphire, and like ruby, it is colored by smaller amounts of chromium, producing a pale pink tone.

LEGENDARY USES

Historically, pink sapphire was considered to be a pale ruby, a softer, lighter version of ruby's passionate intensity. In medieval Europe, nobles and royalty wore the stone to alert them to possible poisoning: if the stone grew dark or cloudy, then evil was close by. It would only resume its pink color once the danger had passed. Not only was the wearer or carrier of this precious stone protected from all evils, but if a stone was placed in each of the four corners of a house, garden or vineyard, the area would be preserved from "lightning, tempests, and worms."

ATTRIBUTES AND POWERS

Pink sapphire is a stone of emotional and psychic protection, one that also promotes determination and emotional courage. This beautiful crystal calms and soothes your heart and soul, and prevents you from "over-thinking" or seeing what you want to see in a romantic situation. With this stone you will always see the truth. Pink sapphire also heals past wounds and encourages compassion for others. Wearing or carrying the stone enhances your ability to be open about relationships and find joy in interacting with others. It enhances intuitive power, and acts as a magnet, drawing into your life romantic opportunities or lovers or partners who will help you evolve and grow into your true potential.

HOW TO USE

Wear or carry pink sapphire to manifest joyful relationships and committed partners.

SUGILITE

APPEARANCE/COLOR: *Shades of purple, violet, pink*

CURRENT AVAILABILITY: *Rare, but available from specialty stores*

PHYSIOLOGICAL CORRESPONDENCE: *Nervous system*

PSYCHOLOGICAL CORRESPONDENCE: *Alleviates sorrow, promotes forgiveness*

ASSOCIATED CRYSTALS BY COLOR: *Charoite, polite*

KEYWORDS: *Spiritual love; deep connection with others*

THE CRYSTAL

Sugilite is a cyclosilicate mineral, crystallizing in a hexagonal system with prismatic crystals, although it is usually found as a mass. Mostly found in Japan and Canada, the best deposits of this violet stone come from very deep manganese mines in South Africa. Other common names of this stone include luvulite and lavulite.

LEGENDARY USES

Since sugilite was only first recorded in 1944, it has no ancient legends or lore associated with it. However, it became very popular in the 1980s, when it was known under its tradename Luvulite. The New Age market discovered its high vibration resonated with the coming "Age of Aquarius" and harnessed its energy to promote all forms of spiritual love. It was thought wearing the stone would enable you to recall your soul's true purpose, and to adapt to being in this incarnation. More recently it has become associated with self-love and forgiveness toward self and others.

ATTRIBUTES AND POWERS

Sugilite promotes love for self and others, and to let go of sorrow, frustration, past angers, and fear. It brings light and love into the darkest of situations, and fills you with joyful trust in the future. By enabling you to accept the "here and now," sugilite instills confidence and a sense of freedom in personal relationships. Wearing or carrying sugilite creates an awareness that one is walking down the right pathway in life. Pink sugilite is a powerful love crystal and when worn as jewelry will attract kindred spirits and soulmates. The stone also dissolves unnecessary sentimentality in relationships, encouraging commitment in good times and bad.

HOW TO USE

Sugilite is best worn or carried to discover a deep bond with another like-minded soul.

TUGTUPITE

APPEARANCE/COLOR: *Red, white, pink*

CURRENT AVAILABILITY: *Rare and fairly expensive*

PHYSIOLOGICAL CORRESPONDENCE: *Blood circulation*

PSYCHOLOGICAL CORRESPONDENCE: *Emotional security*

ASSOCIATED CRYSTALS BY COLOR: *Kunzite, red calcite*

KEYWORDS: *Protects from other's anger; romantic change for the better*

THE CRYSTAL

Tugtupite is rare, and found primarily in, and named for, the region of Tugtup in Greenland. Tugtupite, meaning "reindeer blood stone" is similar in structure to sodalite (see page 156) and occurs in igneous rocks. The stone is tenebrescent, meaning its minerals are capable of changing color when exposed to sunlight.

LEGENDARY USES

Known to the Inuit peoples for thousands of years, there are several legends surrounding tugtupite and its ability to change color. One tells of how a female reindeer herder went into the mountains to give birth. As her blood fell, tugtupite formed and the stone was sacred ever after. Another legend tells that lovers turn the stone bright red with the fire of their passion, and that the stone stimulates the libido, and awakens forgotten love.

ATTRIBUTES AND POWERS

The stone helps you to develop self-love, and teaches you emotional independence, so rather than blame others for your reactions, you learn to own them. The stone transforms bitterness or anger into creative feelings. Wearing the stone means you can accept that romance changes and if you truly want love to start afresh or to be totally different, then you can now manifest those desires.

HOW TO USE

Wear as jewelry to really instill the magic of this stone into your heart chakra and to exude the right kind of romantic desire.

UNAKITE

APPEARANCE/COLOR: *Various shades of green and pinkish red*

CURRENT AVAILABILITY: *Widely available*

PHYSIOLOGICAL CORRESPONDENCE: *Skin, hair*

PSYCHOLOGICAL CORRESPONDENCE: *Personal growth*

ASSOCIATED CRYSTALS BY COLOR: *Green beryl, pink agate*

KEYWORDS: *Togetherness, harmonious relating*

THE CRYSTAL

Unakite is an altered granite and takes its name from the Unaka mountain range in North Carolina where it was first discovered. Composed of green epidote, pink feldspar, and colorless quartz, it also occurs in Africa, Brazil, and China, and is often found in glacial drift, including the deposits found around Lake Superior.

LEGENDARY USES

The green epidote is the dominant mineral in unakite and its name derives from the Greek word *epidosis*, meaning "addition" or "growing together." It is the blend of minerals that convey the stone's symbolic maxim: "That which comes together, belongs together." Brazilian legends claim that anyone who carries the stone will be able to find things that have been lost. The stone can be found as pebbles on the shores of Lake Superior, where indigenous shamans used them to ensure success in casting magic spells.

ATTRIBUTES AND POWERS

The blend and union of the two elements symbolize strong, harmonious relationships. Its pink and green energies balance aspects of the heart, lifting spirits and helping to release negativity. Unakite fosters healthy relationships through balanced emotions. Encouraging harmonious partnerships, both in love and in business, it is especially helpful for working closely with partners, lovers, or friends, where positive personal interactions are vital. The stone promotes self-confidence, strengthens courage, and enhances your ability to bestow love and compassion on others as well as on yourself.

HOW TO USE

Carry with you to manifest harmony and attract good communication in all your relationships, both romantic and business-oriented.

WATERMELON TOURMALINE

APPEARANCE/COLOR: *Pink enfolded in green*

CURRENT AVAILABILITY: *Common*

PHYSIOLOGICAL CORRESPONDENCE: *Nervous system*

PSYCHOLOGICAL CORRESPONDENCE: *Self-expression, heals emotional wounds*

ASSOCIATED CRYSTALS BY COLOR: *Pink tourmaline, rose quartz*

KEYWORDS: *Unconditional loving and acceptance, sexual harmony*

THE CRYSTAL

Tourmalines are aluminum borosilicates that contain such metals as manganese and iron, which account for the huge variation in color across the group and often within a single specimen. The aptly named watermelon tourmaline is colored pink, white, and green within the same crystal. One of the stone's most distinguishing properties is that it is pyroelectric: that is, it has the ability to become electrically charged simply by heating or rubbing it. One end becomes positive and the other negative, allowing it to attract particles of dust.

LEGENDARY USES

Urban legends abound concerning a belief that tourmaline wands are being created in alchemical laboratories deep in the Andes. The enlightened beings who perform this magic charge the wands with cosmic power, which then "appear" in South American mines. These perfectly terminated wands may be a foot long and contain the full color spectrum. Vibrating simultaneously to all the chakras, they align our consciousness directly with universal knowledge. Once mined, these wands attract themselves to those who intuitively know how to use them.

ATTRIBUTES AND POWERS

A favorite among the tourmalines, the so-called watermelon variety is considered to energize and revitalize the heart chakra. While its pink layer is associated with love and emotional happiness, its green layer is beneficial to one's physical being. Together they bring true joy to physical relationships. Wearing or carrying the stone cleanses you of destructive feelings and old wounds. It releases guilt, worry, depression, and anxieties, and diverts those emotions into self-love. It gives the emotionally inert a chance to recover their passion and zest for life, and helps the timid find the courage to love. The stone inspires new trust in others, and manifests happiness, joy, peace, and contentment.

HOW TO USE

Obtain four wands. Place one pointing directly to the west, one to the east, one to the north, and one to the south—all from a central spot. Leave for one lunar cycle to work its magic to manifest love, sexual compatibility, or attract others to you.

ZIRCON

APPEARANCE/COLOR: *Colorless, soft yellow, or pink*

CURRENT AVAILABILITY: *Widely available*

PHYSIOLOGICAL CORRESPONDENCE: *Liver and gallbladder*

PSYCHOLOGICAL CORRESPONDENCE: *Serenity, peace*

ASSOCIATED CRYSTALS BY COLOR: *Yellow sapphire, pink tourmaline*

KEYWORDS: *Attracts new love, romance and harmony*

THE CRYSTAL

Not to be confused with another diamond substitute, cubic zirconia, zircon is the mineral known as zirconium silicate. It occurs naturally in various colors—gold, blue, brown, green, and red—but it is the colorless specimens of zircon that are often used as a substitute for diamonds because they have similar properties of brilliance and fire.

LEGENDARY USE

Zircon was known in early Hindu mythology as one of the many gemstones on the mystical, wish-fulfilling kalpa tree—a green variety of zircon was thought to be the tree's foliage. In ancient Greece, zircon was also called hyacinth or jacinth. One legend tells of the mythological youth, Hyacinthus, who was accidentally slain by his lover, the god Apollo. In his grief, Apollo turned the youth's blood into the hyacinth flower, whose beauty was forever after reflected in zircon. Wearing the stone was believed to drive away evil spirits and protect its wearer from enchantment and lightning.

ATTRIBUTES AND POWERS

Wearing or carrying zircon keeps love and romance "vivid," passionate, real, and eternal, and promotes a harmonious loving energy around you to attract and manifest new love. The stone also promotes awareness of your true needs and desires in love, and brings you to a realization that your expectations of others may be too high. Placing zircon in the southwest area of your home will also bring you honest acceptance of how other people have their own dreams and desires too.

HOW TO USE

To bring new love into your life, place six pieces of clear zircon at the points of the shape of a six-pointed star. Light a pink candle in the middle and say: "Let unconditional love flow between myself and someone new. I call on my soulmate to lovingly manifest in my life." Focus on the crystals for a few minutes before you blow out the candle to "fire" your intention to the universe.

FURTHER READING

BOOKS

Fernie, William T. *The Occult and Curative Powers of Precious Stones.* New York: Rudolf Steiner Publications, 1973.

Hall, Judy. *The Crystal Bible: A Definitive Guide to Crystals.* Arlesford, UK: Godsfield Press, 2003.

——. *Crystal Healing.* Arlesford, UK: Godsfield Press, 2005.

——. *101 Power Crystals: The Ultimate Guide to Magical Crystals, Gems, and Stones for Healing and Transformation.* Beverly, MA, USA: Fair Winds Press, 2011.

Kunz, George Frederick, *The Curious Lore of Precious Stones.* 1913. Reprint, New York: Dover Publications, 1971.

Raphaell, Katrina. *Crystal Enlightenment: The Transforming Properties of Crystals and Healing Stones.* Santa Fe, NM, USA: Aurora Press, 1985.

Simmons, Robert. *The Pocket Book of Stones: Who They Are & What They Teach: Revised & Expanded Edition.* Berkeley, CA, USA: North Atlantic Books, 2015.

Virtue, Doreen and Judith Lukomski. *Crystal Therapy: How to Heal and Empower Your Life with Crystal Energy.* London, UK: Hay House Publishing, 2005.

WEBSITES

The Astrology Room
www.theastrologyroom.com

The Crystal Healer
www.thecrystalhealer.co.uk

Crystalinks
www.crystalinks.com

Crystal Vaults
www.crystalvaults.com

Emily Gems
www.crystal-cure.com

HealingCrystals.com
www.healingcrystals.com

Judy Hall
www.judyhall.co.uk

GLOSSARY

ANIMISM
A belief that a spiritual or divine essence, or "soul," permeates all things—rocks, trees, plants, and animals.

ARCHETYPE
A universal energy or pattern of behavior which operates autonomously in the depths of the human psyche.

ASTROLOGY
An ancient system of divination which studies the patterns and placement of the planets of the solar system as they appear to travel through the zodiac belt.

BAGUA
The magical compass used in the ancient Chinese art of feng shui. It can be used to determine which areas of your home to place certain crystals for harmony and enhancement.

CHAKRA
A spinning vortex of invisible energy with seven or more "centers" throughout the body.

DEDICATION
The quality of being committed to a purpose. In the case of dedicating a crystal, this means ensuring that a crystal's sole task is to help you fulfil your particular goal.

EARTH ACUPUNCTURE

The practice of burying crystals in the ground or laying them in a grid system, in order to create balance and harmony in the environment.

ELECTROMAGNETIC ENERGY

Energy that is emitted or reflected by objects in the form of electrical and magnetic waves.

FENG SHUI

The ancient Chinese art of placement and balance in the home and/or environment to ensure good business, harmony, love, and success.

GEMSTONE

(also known as gem, semiprecious or precious stone, or jewel)
A piece of mineral which, in cut and polished form, is used to make jewelry or other adornments. The most well-known precious gemstones are diamonds, rubies, emeralds, and sapphires. Rare minerals such as lapis lazuli are also used for jewelry and are often considered to be precious gemstones too but are classified, like most other crystals, as semiprecious stones.

GEOMANCY

An ancient form of divination in which the marks and patterns of stones, earth, and sand on the ground were "read." In the Renaissance, it was popularized by occultists such as Cornelius Agrippa as a symbolic form of divination magic.

GEOPATHIC STRESS

A type of energy created by disturbances and negative power from underground water courses, power lines, and negative ley lines (Earth energy). This energy runs through, under, or above the ground and can pollute and influence people and buildings.

GRIDDING

The placing of crystals in specific patterns on a table or around a building, room, outdoor place or person's body for enhancement or protection.

GROUNDING

A way of creating and balancing one's own personal energy to gain a firm sense of connectedness to the Earth.

HOLY GRAIL

A legendary relic originating in medieval Christian mythology. The Grail was thought to be the cup which contained the blood of Jesus from his crucifixion.

MAGMA

From a Greek word meaning "thick" and "unguent," magma is a mixture of molten or semi-molten rock, gases, and solids that is found beneath the surface of the Earth.

ORACLE

A message that was sent by ancient Greek gods, such as Apollo, and transmitted through a high priestess at the god's temple. It was originally advice or a prediction about an individual's future. The word is used today in various divination techniques to describe an individual's present and future.

PENDULUM DOWSING

A method of divination which uses a pendulum, usually made of crystal or precious metal, to locate missing objects or to give answers to specific questions. The pendulum can also be used to dowse for geopathic stress.

PIEZOELECTRIC EFFECT

Discovered by French physicist and chemist Pierre Curie (1859–1906), this is the ability of certain materials to create an electric charge when pressure or stress is applied to them. For instance, by squeezing a crystal a voltage is produced across the crystal's surface.

PROGRAMMING

A term used to describe how to focus specific energy into a crystal so that it continues to promote the energy of your chosen desire.

QUANTUM PHYSICS

The science that deals with the nature and behavior of matter and energy on the atomic and subatomic scale. It is the study of photons, electrons, and other such particles which make up the universe.

REINFORCING STONES

Crystals which strengthen or support specific chakras. These stones help to restore energy to a specific chakra energy center.

RESONANCE

A sympathetic vibration between people, objects, symbols, or qualities, as well as between the crystals you choose and the purpose they are used for.

SPREAD

A layout or pattern of stones placed in a specific order to create a symbolic matrix for divination.

SUBDUING STONES

Bringing under control any excess or confused energy in the chakras or psyche. These stones bring calm and restore balance to overactive energy centres

SYMBOL
A sign, mark, image, or code which represents something else.

TAROT
A deck of 78 mystical cards, which are symbolic of the archetypal nature of the universe.

TUMBLED
Stones that have been polished in a large drum with grit to give them a smooth and often shiny finish.

UNIVERSAL ENERGY
The energy of the universe which, according to some belief systems, permeates and connects all things. Also known as the Anima Mundi in Neoplatonic systems of thought, *chi* by the ancient Chinese Taoists, *prana* in Hindu, and *mana* in Polynesian cultures.

VIBRATIONAL ENERGY
According to quantum physics, everything in the universe vibrates at different or varying speeds, including the wavelengths of the electromagnetic spectrum.

ZODIAC
An imaginary belt that lies along the ecliptic (the apparent pathway of the sun), made up of 12 equal, 30-degree segments of a circle, known as the twelve signs of the zodiac.

INDEX

CREDITS